BREAK THE LANGUAGE BARRIER LEVEL 3
WWW.ELPRINCIPECENTRE.COM
info@elprincipecentre.org

INTRODUCTION

If you have chosen this book to help you learn Spanish you will have either already completed Levels 1 and/ or 2 or will have felt that your level of Spanish was sufficient to start here at Level 3. Level 3 assumes knowledge and confidence with present and past tenses and I would not recommend starting this course without this. Pronunciation tutorials are available on my YouTube channel https://youtu.be/fRH-q7OIGaU. Subscription is totally free.

If you find difficulty from the beginning, it would be a good idea to start with Level 1 or 2 for the good foundations they will give you. Here in Level 3 we will continue with the most important past tenses, and learn to express ourselves in the future, future conditional and imperative along with those pesky pronouns and solving the mysteries of "por" versus "para". My method of teaching Spanish is all about communication rather than grammatical perfection. I have chosen the elements I believe are necessary to communicate effectively in Spanish. I do not delve into grammatical aspects that are too confusing and not necessary to get your point across. I concentrate on those components that will help successfully achieve whatever it is you are trying to do.

However, I do not advocate "phrasebook" Spanish or "holiday" Spanish. With my method you will learn how to take the various components of the language in the simplest form possible and build your own phrases and questions to leave you confident in any situation. Spanish is a lovely, rich language spoken widely throughout the world. Most importantly, I hope you will enjoy working through this Level and feel sufficiently confident at the end to cope with anything. The past tenses in particular can be notoriously difficult to get to grips with, and you will learn a lot about your own language as you work through them. It goes without saying that being able to use past and future tenses with confidence will expand your communication options immensely.

Accept with good grace that instant perfection is too much to expect, learn from your mistakes and be bold as you try to understand and make yourself understood. That is all part of the fun of learning a new language!!

Suerte!!

Vicki

BREAK THE LANGUAGE BARRIER LEVEL 3
WWW.ELPRINCIPECENTRE.COM
info@elprincipecentre.org

INDEX

	PAGE
1. CUÉNTANOS DE TÍ.	4
2. SUMMARY OF PAST TENSES.	5
3. MIXED TENSE CONVERSATION PRACTICE.	7
4. TRANSLATION AND PRESENT AND PAST TENSES.	8
5. FUTURE- "GOING TO".	11
6. FUTURE- "WILL".	14
7. FUTURE TENSE IN CONTEXT.	18
8. FUTURE SIMPLE-THE NEW HOUSE	21
9. FUTURE SIMPLE IRREGULAR VERBS	23
10. CONDITIONAL.	25
11. FUTURE/ CONDITIONAL/ CONVERSATION PRACTICE	28
12. "SER" AND "ESTAR"- FUTURE/ CONDITIONAL.	29
13. DEMONSTRATIVE ADJECTIVES AND PRONOUNS.	30
14. INDIRECT OBJECT PRONOUNS.	32
15. POSSESSIVE ADJECTIVES AND PRONOUNS	35
16. VERB TABLES	37
17. "PARA" OR "POR"?- PART I- "PARA".	42
18. "PARA" OR "POR"?- PART II- "POR".	44
19. "PARA" OR "POR"?- COMPARISON A.	47
20. "PARA" OR "POR"?- COMPARISON B.	48
21. PARA" OR "POR"?- COMPARISON C.	49
22. TRANSLATION ENGLISH TO SPANISH MIXED TENSES.	50
23. THE IMPERATIVE OR "COMMAND" MODE I- "TÚ"-	53
24. THE IMPERATIVE "TÚ"- IRREGULAR VERBS.	55
25. THE IMPERATIVE "TÚ"- PLACEMENT OF PRONOUNS.	56
26. THE IMPERATIVE OR "COMMAND" MODE II- "VOSOTROS".	57
27. IMPERATIVE SUMMARY	59
28. PRACTICE THE IMPERATIVE	60
29. PRONOUN PRACTICE	61
30. PRACTICE OF PERSONAL PRONOUNS	62
31. SER V ESTAR MIXED TENSES	64
32. JUAN PEREZ´S MEXICAN ADVENTURE	69
33. QUERIDA PILI	72
34. PREPOSITIONS	76

	PAGE
35. CONVERSATION TRANSLATION PALOMA/ JUAN	79
36. EMAILS	80
37. POSTSCRIPT	81
38. KEY TO "TOP TIPS".	82
39. ANSWERS.	83

1. CUÉNTANOS DE TÍ.

If you are ready for Level 3, you should be able to ask and answer the following questions in Spanish with relative ease. ☺ If you have problems with these, please go back through Level 2 to refresh before starting this course.

PRACTICE A: Translate these questions into Spanish and answer them appropriately.

1. Where did you live before coming to Spain?
2. What did you used to do?
3. Do you work now?
4. What is your partner like?
5. Do you have any pets?
6. Why and when did you come to Spain?
7. How have you practised Spanish since your last class?
8. What bad experiences have you had in Spain?
9. How long have you studied Spanish?
10. Did you go on holiday last year?
11. What advice do you have for the other students in order to learn Spanish well?
12. What are the biggest problems that you have had in learning Spanish?
13. What do you want to achieve after this course?
14. When was the last time that you spoke Spanish?

Top Tips!!

1. "IR A" OR "IR DE"?

As we in saw in Level 1 of this course, the verb "ir" is nearly always accompanied by "a" as we are usually going "to" somewhere. Two exceptions to this are "to go on holiday" which translates to "ir de vacaciones", and "to go shopping" which is "ir de compras".

E.g. **Fui de vacaciones el año pasado**- I went on holiday last year.
   Siempre íbamos de compras los sábados- We always went shopping on Saturdays.

2. SUMMARY OF PAST TENSES.

1. THE PRESENT PERFECT.

Compound tense- straddles 2 time zones- used for actions that started in the past and are still continuing or very recent past actions- translates to "to have done" something.

Formation:

A. To have (use "haber", not "tener")

he - I have / I´ve
has - you have/ you´ve
ha - he/she/it has- he´s/she´s/it´s
hemos- we have/ we´ve
habéis- you(s) have/ you´ve
han- they have/ they´ve

B. Past participle of the second verb, i.e the action that we "have done". Regular **past participles** :

"**Ar**" verbs- remove the "ar" and add "**ado**", i.e **hablado- spoken**
"**Er**" verbs- remove the "er" and add "**ido**", i.e **aprendido- learnt**
"**Ir**" verbs-same as "er" verbs, i.e **vivido- lived**

C. Irregular participles:

escribir-escrito, hacer-hecho, romper-roto, ver-visto, volver-vuelto, decir-dicho, abrir-abierto, morir-muerto, poner-puesto, cubrir-cubierto, freir-frito.

2. THE PAST PERFECT.

Translates to "had" done something.

Formation: Also compound tense.
A: Use past imperfect tense of "haber"

había- I had/ I´d
habías- you had/ you´d
había- he/she/it had-he´d, she´d, it´d

habíamos- we had/ we´d
habíais-you(s) had/ you´d
habían- they had/ they´d

B: Past Participle as "Present Perfect" above.

BREAK THE LANGUAGE BARRIER LEVEL 3
WWW.ELPRINCIPECENTRE.COM
info@elprincipecentre.org

3. THE PRETERITE.

Singular, completed actions in the past, at a specific point in time. In English, anything we 'did'.

A: Regular verbs:

"Ar" verbs- é, aste, ó, amos, asteis, aron
"Er/ ir" verbs- í, iste, ió, imos, isteis, ieron

B: Irregular verbs:

* hacer- hic	tener -tuv
poner- pus	*decir - dij
poder-pud	*conducir- conduj
saber -sup	*traer - traj
estar - estuv	querer - quis
* dar - d	venir- vin

Endings – e, iste, o, imos, isteis, ieron (except dar-takes the endings for **REGULAR** "er" verbs but no accents)

C: "Ser"/ "Ir"- fui, fuiste, fue, fuimos, fuisteis, fueron.

4. THE IMPERFECT.

Past repeated actions or actions with no specific beginning or end- background descriptions in the past-things we "were doing" or "used to do". Most verbs are regular in this tense.

A: Regular verbs

"Ar"- aba, abas, aba, ábamos, abais, aban
"Er"/ "ir" - ía, ías, ía, íamos, íais, ían

B: There are only 3 irregular verbs in this tense:

"**Ser**": era, eras, era, éramos, erais, eran
"**Ver**": veía, veías, veía, veíamos, veíais, veían
"**Ir**": iba, ibas, iba, íbamos, ibais, iban

3. MIXED TENSE CONVERSATION PRACTICE.

PRACTICE A: Translate these questions into Spanish paying careful attention to the tense of the verb. Practice asking and answering them with a partner.

1. What did you do last night?
2. Have you ever done anything silly?
3. Have you ever written a poem?
4. When you were a child did you have any animals?
5. What did you want to be?
6. Where did you go the day before yesterday?
7. Have you ever studied German?
8. Who did you speak to on Saturday?
9. Did you always do your homework at school?
10. Have you ever had an accident?
11. What did you put on yesterday?
12. Where was your first house?
13. What colour was your first car?
14. When did you have your first Spanish class?
15. Why did you come to Spain?
16. What time did you go to bed last Monday?
17. Did you have a shower yesterday?
18. Have you ever had a dog?
19. Have you ever met anyone famous?
20. Who did you see at the weekend?
21. What was the last book that you read?
22. Have you ever won a prize?
23. Could you speak Spanish before coming here?
24. When you were a child did you know how to swim?
25. When did you use to go on holiday?
26. Have you ever lost all your money?

4. TRANSLATION AND COMPREHENSION PRACTICE PRESENT AND PAST TENSES.

PRACTICE A: Pick out the 46 verbs in this text and use them to complete the verb table below as per the example.

Paco and José **were sitting** in a car outside the bank in the main street. They were both policemen but they were not wearing uniforms and they were in Paco´s little grey car. They had heard that someone was going to rob the bank. They were beside the pavement on the other side of the street. It was 8 o´clock in the morning. The bank had not opened yet and there weren´t many people on the street.
"Is it today?" said Paco.
"That´s what they told me" said José. "They´ve always told me the truth. We must wait at least an hour, then we can go home."

They waited till 8.30. The bank opened, and many people entered. At 8.45 a black van parked outside. Two men got out of the van and entered the bank.

"I think it´s them" said Paco, and they called for assistance.

The police entered the bank 5 minutes later and the robbery had already started. The men were carrying guns and they had made all the customers lie down on the floor with their hands behind their head. The cashiers were putting the money in bags to give to the robbers. The police immediately arrested the 2 men without problems and Paco and José spoke to them before leaving.

"You have done well", they told them. "Let´s go to the station with them now and then we can go home".

VERB	INFINITIVE	SPANISH	TENSE	PERSON
1. were sitting	To sit	sentarse	imperfect	3rd p.plural
2.				
3.				
4.				
5.				
6.				
7.				
8.				
9.				

10.				
11.				
12.				
13.				
14.				
15.				
16.				
17.				
18.				
19.				
20.				
21.				
22.				
23.				
24.				
25.				
26.				
27.				
28.				
29.				
30.				
31.				
32.				
33.				
34.				
35.				
36.				
37.				
38.				
39.				
40.				
41.				
42.				
43.				
44.				
45.				
46.				

PRACTICE B: Translate the text into Spanish.

PRACTICE C: Translate the questions into Spanish then answer in Spanish.

1. Where were Paco and José sitting?
2. What were they?
3. Were they wearing uniforms?
4. Which car were they in?
5. What had they heard?
6. Where were they?
7. What time was it?
8. Had the bank opened?
9. Were there many people in the street?
10. How long must they wait?
11. What can they do then?
12. Until what time did they wait?
13. What happened when the bank opened?
14. What happened at 8.45?
15. What did the two men do?
16. What did Paco and José do?
17. When did the police enter the bank?
18. What had happened inside?
19. What were the men carrying?
20. What had they made the customers do?
21. What were the cashiers doing?
22. What did the police do immediately?
23. Who did Paco and José speak to before leaving?
24. What did they all do then?

Top Tips!!

---

2. "BIEN" OR "BUENO/A?"

It is easy to get confused over whether to use "bien" o "bueno" as they can both translate to "good". "Bien" is an adverb, used to describe a verb, (how one does something) wheras "bueno" is an adjective and therefore used to describe a noun.
E.g. He is a good dancer- **Es bailador bueno.**
He dances well- **Baila bien.**
He disfrutado mucho la fiesta, ha sido muy buena- I have enjoyed the party very much, it has been very good.
Lo he pasado muy bien en la fiesta- I have had a good time at the party.

5. FUTURE- "GOING TO".

The first and simplest way of expressing the future in Spanish requires the use of the verb 'ir' in the present tense, plus 'a', plus the infinitive of the verb expressing what we are going to do.

PRESENT TENSE "IR"-

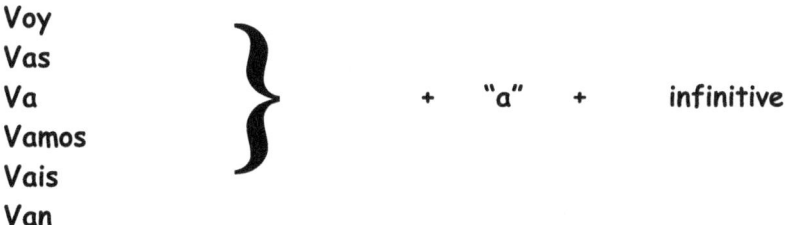

Voy
Vas
Va
Vamos
Vais
Van

} + "a" + infinitive

E.g.
Voy a comprar un coche nuevo en enero- **I'm going to buy** a new car in January.
Vamos a vender nuestra casa el año que viene- **We're going to sell** our house next year.

PRACTICE A: Translate into Spanish.

1. What are you(s) going to do at Christmas?
2. They are going to visit Sevilla in May.
3. Luis is going to give up smoking one day.
4. I am going to tell him the truth.
5. Are you going to go to the party?
6. It is going to be very difficult.
7. We are not going to be happy.
8. Are they going to make dinner or not?
9. When are you going to do it?
10. They are going to want a lot of things.
11. Carmen is going to get up early tomorrow.
12. I am not going to buy it yet.
13. My parents are going to be very angry.
14. They are not going to be very happy.
15. The dogs are going to be hungry later.

BREAK THE LANGUAGE BARRIER LEVEL 3
WWW.ELPRINCIPECENTRE.COM
info@elprincipecentre.org

PRACTICE B: Find the 32 verbs in this text and use them to complete the verb table below as per the example.

Tomorrow is my sister's birthday. I am going to have a party for her. I am going to invite lots of people because I have a big house. I have lots of parties and I always do something special. I normally buy a cake and I am going to tell the baker that I want lots of flowers and my sister's name on the cake. He is going to make a very special cake for her and he is going to deliver it tomorrow morning. All my sister's friends are going to come to the party and they are going to bring presents and flowers for her. We are going to have lots of games and music, and her boyfriend is going to make lots of cocktails. We are going to enjoy it and my sister is going to be really surprised and happy. I know that she isn't going to be angry with me for planning it without her permission.

VERB	INFINITIVE	SPANISH	TENSE	PERSON
1. is	To be	ser	present	1st p.sing
2.				
3.				
4.				
5.				
6.				
7.				
8.				
9.				
10.				
11.				
12.				
13.				
14.				
15.				
16.				
17.				
18.				
19.				
20.				
21.				
22.				
23.				
24.				

25.				
26.				
27.				
28.				
29.				
30.				
31.				
32.				

PRACTICE C: Translate the text into Spanish.

PRACTICE D: Translate these questions into Spanish and answer in Spanish from the text.

1. What day is it tomorrow?
2. What is she going to have?
3. Why is she going to invite a lot of people?
4. What does she always do?
5. What does she normally buy?
6. What is she going to tell the baker?
7. What is he going to make and when is he going to deliver it?
8. Who are going to come to the party?
9. What are they going to bring?
10. What are they going to have?
11. What is her sister´s boyfriend going to make?
12. Are they going to enjoy it?
13. How is her sister going to be?
14. Is she going to be angry for planning it without her permission?

Top Tips!!

3."GENTE"- PEOPLE.

The word "gente" that means "people" in Spanish is feminine and singlar, often causing confusion as it doesn´t end in "a" and should never be made plural by ending an "s".

E.g: There were a lot of people- Había mucha gente.
People want to shop on Sundays- La gente quiere ir de compras los domingos.
There are a lot of good people in the world- Hay mucha gente buena en el mundo.

6. FUTURE- "WILL".

REGULAR VERBS.

The future tense is one of the easiest tenses to learn as the endings are the same for all conjugations. For regular verbs, they are simply tagged on to the infinitive. However, the pronunciation can be tricky!!
Regular verbs are conjugated as follows:

hablar	**comer**	**vivir**
hablar **é**	comer **é**	vivir **é**
hablar **ás**	comer **ás**	vivir **ás**
hablar **á**	comer **á**	vivir **á**
hablar **emos**	comer **emos**	vivir **emos**
hablar **éis**	comer **éis**	vivir **éis**
hablar **án**	comer **án**	vivir **án**

PRACTICE A: Translate into Spanish.

1. I will live in my own house soon.
2. Where will you go on Saturday?
3. I won't take him again.
4. When will she see him again?
5. They'll never buy a house.
6. We will never eat in this restaurant again.
7. I will speak Spanish all the time in class.
8. He will work for a bank in Santander.
9. I will enjoy my holidays next month.
10. She will get up at 6 o clock in the morning tomorrow.
11. We will spend all day on the beach.
12. They will go to the cinema on Thursday.
13. He won´t leave her in peace.
14. When will you(s) return to England?
15. Will you stay in a hotel?
16. They said they will go to the party.
17. I won´t buy anything at the market.
18. I will wash my hair tonight.
19. They will study Spanish 3 times a week.
20. Will you have a shower tonight or in the morning?

BREAK THE LANGUAGE BARRIER LEVEL 3
WWW.ELPRINCIPECENTRE.COM
info@elprincipecentre.org

IRREGULAR VERBS.

With irregular verbs, the endings are the same but the stem changes.

<u>Tener</u> -to have

Tendr **é** - I will have
Tendr **ás** - you will have
Tendr **á** -he/she/it will have
Tendr **emos** - we will have
Tendr **éis**- you(s) will have
Tendr **án**- they will have

E.g. **Tendré los libros mañana**- I will have the books tomorrow.
Tendremos una clase de español la semana que viene- We will have a Spanish class next week.

PRACTICE B: Find the meaning of the verbs below and conjugate them.

1. **saber**- sabr
2. **venir**-vendr
3. **querer**- querr
4. **poner**- pondr
5. **decir**- dir
6. **haber**- habr
7. **poder**- podr
8. **salir**- saldr
9. **hacer**- har
10. **caber**-cabr
11. **valer**- valdr

PRACTICE C: Use them to translate these sentences.

1. When will you know?
2. There will be some refreshments.
3. What will he say to them?
4. I will do the plan tomorrow.
5. They will have the contract next week.
6. I will want a cup of tea later.
7. What time will he come?
8. Will you(s) put the games in the cupboard later?
9. We will not be able to go to the party on Friday.
10. Will it fit in that corner?
11. His plane will leave at 10 o'clock.
12. What will they be worth next year?

PRACTICE D: Complete the sentences below using any verb in the future tense.

1. El año que viene ...
2. Pasado mañana ...
3. La semana que viene...
4. En mi cumpleaños ...
5. En Navidad ...
6. En verano ...
7. Mañana por la mañana ...
8. En mayo ...
9. La próxima vez que voy a mi país ...
10. Este sábado por la noche ...

PRACTICE E: Pick out the 30 verbs in this text and use them to complete the table below as per the example.

In a couple of months **_I will leave_** my job and I will go to live in Spain. I will sell everything that I own and I will start a new life. I have saved enough money (in order) to live for 10 years if I am careful. I won´t be able to buy lots of things but I will spend more time with my family and we will be able to travel around Spain. We will visit new places and we will meet new people.

I will get up late and I will go to bed late. I won´t always have to look at the clock. I will go to the beach in the day and I will sit outside in the evening. When I want to, I will drink wine. I won´t have a big house and a big car, I won´t be able to buy lots of clothes or expensive things but I will be happy. For the first time, my reality and my dreams will be the same. I won´t want much, just the simple pleasures of life.

VERB	INFINITIVE	SPANISH	TENSE	PERSON
1. I will leave	To leave	dejar	future	1st p. sing
2.				
3.				
4.				
5.				
6.				
7.				
8.				
9.				
10.				

11.				
12.				
13.				
14.				
15.				
16.				
17.				
18.				
19.				
20.				
21.				
22.				
23.				
24.				
25.				
26.				
27.				
28.				
29.				
30.				

PRACTICE F: Translate the text into Spanish.

 Top Tips!!

4. "YA".

"Ya" is a very useful little word in Spanish that can translate to "now", "already", "later", and even a sarcastic and sardonic "yes". It can often transmit a sense of impatience or irritation when it is used, and sometimes surprise.

E.g:

Ya lo sé- I already know.
Tienes que hacerlo ya.- You have to do it (right) now.
¿Lo han hecho ya?- Have they already done it?
Ya tengo suficiente.- I have had enough now.
Ya, ya, y los cerdos vuelen.- Yes, of course, and pigs can fly.
Vamos a las tiendas ya.- We are going to the shops now/later.

7. FUTURE TENSE IN CONTEXT.

PRACTICE A: Practice reading this text out loud.

PEDRO: Hola Juan. Hay dos correos electrónicos en el ordenador para tí.
JUAN: Ah, éste es de José. Salió de vacaciones hace cinco días para Inglaterra. A ver que nos cuenta ... Dice que hace mucho frio pero se divierte mucho. También dice que ha conocido a una chica inglesa muy simpática. Dice que mañana saldrán para el norte y que visitarán algunos pueblos del campo juntos.
PEDRO: Ah, me acuerdo cuando trabajaba yo con José en el banco.
¿Cuándo volverá?
JUAN: Creo que llegará a Barcelona el sábado que viene.
PEDRO: ¿Lo acompañará esa inglesa que ha conocido?
JUAN: Dice que la ha invitado, pero no sabe si aceptará, aunque cree que está interesada. La conoció el primer día de las vacaciones.
PEDRO: ¡Qué suerte estar de vacaciones! Yo no podré irme hasta el mes que viene. ¿Y tú?
JUAN: Yo también tendré mis vacaciones en agosto. Iré a Londrés para ver si tendré tanta suerte como José.
PEDRO: Es buena idea. A lo mejor te acompañaré.
JUAN: Un momento! El otro correo electrónico es de mi tía Juana. Me dice que me dará quinientos euros para mi cumpleaños. Te invito yo. Vamos a celebrarlo. ¿Qué te parece tomar unas copas?
PEDRO: Estupendo!

PRACTICE B: Pick out the 47 verbs and put them into the verb identification table below as per the first 3 examples.

VERB	INFINITIVE	ENGLISH	TENSE	PERSON
1. hay	haber	There are	present simple	3 p.sing.
2. es	ser	To be	present	3 p.sing.
3. salió	salir	To leave	preterite	3 p.sing.
4.				
5.				
6.				
7.				
8.				
9.				

10.				
11.				
12.				
13.				
14.				
15.				
16.				
17.				
18.				
19.				
20.				
21.				
22.				
23.				
24.				
25.				
26.				
27.				
28.				
29.				
30.				
31.				
32.				
33.				
34.				
35.				
36.				
37.				
38.				
39.				
40.				
41.				
42.				
43.				
44.				
45.				
46.				
47.				

PRACTICE C: Translate the text into English.

PRACTICE D: Translate the questions into Spanish and answer in Spanish.

1. How many emails are there for Juan?
2. When did José leave on holiday?
3. Where did he go?
4. What does he say in the email?
5. Who has he met?
6. Where will they leave for tomorrow?
7. Where did Pedro work with José?
8. When will José return?
9. Will the English girl that he has met come with him?
10. When did he meet her?
11. When will Pedro and Juan be able to go on holiday?
12. Where will Juan go?
13. Who will probably go with him?
14. Who is the other email from?
15. How much does she say that she will give him for his birthday?

Top Tips!!

5. "SER" and "ESTAR" - REMEMBER THE DIFFERENCE?

"SER" - "COPPPRINCT"

<u>C</u> OLOURS
<u>O</u> RIGIN
<u>P</u> ROFESSION
<u>P</u> OSSESSION
<u>P</u> ERSONAL
<u>R</u> ELATIONSHIPS
<u>I</u> DENTITY
<u>N</u> ATIONALITY
<u>C</u> HARACTERISTICS
<u>T</u> IME

"ESTAR" - "FLOMMETS"

<u>F</u> EELINGS
<u>L</u>
<u>O</u> CATION
<u>M</u> OODS
<u>M</u> ARITAL STATUS
<u>E</u> MOTIONS
<u>T</u> EMPORARY
<u>S</u> TATES

9. FUTURE SIMPLE: THE NEW HOUSE.

Alberto: I have bought a new house in the country. The town is over there and that house next to the river is mine.
Manuel: How pretty it is!! Will you live here all year?
Alberto: No, for now I will only spend the weekends here. This way and I will show you it, although the reformations are not finished yet. Next week they will install the electricity and the heating.
Manuel: This hallway is really big. How will you furnish it?
Alberto: I will furnish it bit by bit. I haven´t got much money now to buy lots of furniture at once.
Manuel: Will you decorate it yourself?
Alberto: Yes, I will bring some pictures and ornaments from the apartment. Opposite the door, I will place a Spanish dresser, and above, a mirror.
Manuel: This room, will it be the living room?
Alberto: Yes, at the moment I will put a sofa and various chairs. The television will go over there, and in that corner a bar.
Manuel: And which will be your study?
Alberto: That room over there, at the end of the corridor. In front of my work table I will place a big bookcase that will occupy all the wall. The study will connect with my bedroom.
Manuel: I don´t see any fireplace. Will you build one?
Alberto: Of course! It will be in the living room. In winter it will be great to read and chat in front of the fire.
Manuel: I love your house. Will you invite me some time?
Alberto: Of course I will. Here you have your house too.

PRACTICE A: Pick out the 33 verbs and use them to complete the verb recognition table below.

VERB	INFINITIVE	SPANISH	TENSE	PERSON
1.				
2.				
3.				
4.				
5.				
6.				
7.				
8.				
9.				

10.				
11.				
12.				
13.				
14.				
15.				
16.				
17.				
18.				
19.				
20.				
21.				
22.				
23.				
24.				
25.				
26.				
27.				
28.				
29.				
30.				
31.				
32.				
33.				

PRACTICE B: Translate into Spanish.

PRACTICE C: Translate the questions into Spanish and answer in Spanish.

1. Where is Alberto´s new house?
2. Will he live there all year?
3. Are the reformations finished yet?
4. What will they install for him next week?
5. How will he furnish the hallway?
6. Will Alberto call a decorator or will he decorate the house himself?
7. What will he put in the living room?
8. Which will be his study and with which room will it connect?
9. Will he build a fireplace? Where and why?
10. Describe your house.

9. FUTURE SIMPLE-TRANSLATION USING IRREGULAR VERBS.

PEDRO: Hello Carmen, Please can you pack me a suitcase. I have to go on a trip to Paris.
CARMEN: When will you leave?
PEDRO: After lunch I will go to Barcelona and there I will catch the train to Paris.
CARMEN: Will you be in Paris many days?
PEDRO: No, I hope to be there only a couple of days. I will have to discuss a few important things that will only take me a short time. I will come home on Friday and will tell you everything.
CARMEN: Then I will pack the small case for you, it is more comfortable for travelling. Why don´t you go by plane?
PEDRO: No! You know that I dont like to go by plane. It´s dangerous.
CARMEN: You are scared of planes. Then you will go on the sleeper train?
PEDRO: Of course. It is the most comfortable and safe way to travel. I will be able to relax quite a few hours.
CARMEN: Ok, I will bring your case to the office shortly. I´ll see you then.
PEDRO: Good, until then.

PRACTICE A: Pick out the 32 verbs in this passage and use them to fill out the verb identification table below.

VERB	INFINITIVE	SPANISH	TENSE	PERSON
1.				
2.				
3.				
4.				
5.				
6.				
7.				
8.				
9.				
10.				
11.				
12.				
13.				
14.				

15.				
16.				
17.				
18.				
19.				
20.				
21.				
22.				
23.				
24.				
25.				
26.				
27.				
28.				
29.				
30.				
31.				
32.				

PRACTICE B: *Translate into Spanish.*

PRACTICE C: *Translate the questions into Spanish and answer in Spanish.*

1. Does Pedro have to go on a trip?
2. Where will Pedro travel to?
3. When will he leave?
4. Will he spend many days in Paris?
5. What will he have to discuss?
6. When will he come home and what will he do?
7. What will he travel on?
8. What will Carmen pack for him and why?
9. Why won´t he travel by plane?
10. Why does he prefer the train?
11. From where will he go to Paris?
12. To where will Carmen take the case?
13. Where will be the next place you travel to?
14. Will you take a lot of luggage with you?

10. CONDITIONAL.

We use the condtional tense when we want to express uncertainty in the future, and it usually translates to "would" in English.

E.g. We would like to.
I would go on holiday more, but I have no time.
He would go to the party, but he is working.
They would buy the house, but they have to wait.
I would not eat in that restaurant.
Would you buy a new car?

The conditional is similar to the future simple "will" in Spanish as there are few irregular verbs, and in fact the two tenses share the same ones. To conjugate the regular verbs, we use the infinitive as the stem and add on these endings, regardless of whether it is an "ar", "er" or "ir" verb.

- ía, ías, ía, íamos, íais, ían

PRACTICE A: Translate.

1. I would eat the biscuits, but I am on a diet.
2. Would you marry him?
3. Where would you(s) go?
4. They wouldn't live in that house because it's too small.
5. Would you deliver the books to our house?
6. You(s) would be my students.
7. They would lose it.
8. We would sing a song but we have a cold.
9. I'd get up but I'm too comfortable.
10. They know that you would give them the money tomorrow.
11. Why would anybody eat that?
12. Why wouldn't I go to bed at that time?
13. You wouldn't play the piano in front of all those people.
14. They wouldn't pay much for the house.
15. He wouldn't go to bed before 11.
16. I wouldn't have a bath in the summer.

PRACTICE B: IRREGULAR VERBS-The same verbs that were irregular in the future are irregular also in the future conditional. What do these verbs mean and what are their stems? Conjugate them.(The endings are the same as the regular verb endings.)

1. HABER-
2. PODER-
3. QUERER-
4. SABER-
5. PONER-
6. SALIR-
7. TENER-
8. VALER-
9. VENIR-
10. DECIR-
11. HACER-

PRACTICE C: What would you do if you won the lottery? Name 10 things...

1.
2.
3.
4.
5.
6.
7.
8.
9.
10.

PRACTICE D: Pick out the verbs in this text (23) and complete the verb identification table:

When I was young, I loved to read and I had a vivid imagination. One of my favourite characters was the Genie of the Lamp because he could grant people 3 wishes. What would I ask for? First, I would ask him for a hundred more wishes, but I know that he wouldn't do that. Therefore, these would be my 3 wishes. 1. My dog would be able to speak, and she and I would have long conversations. 2. I would marry the man of my dreams. 3. And the most important wish would be easy... no one in the world would have to suffer any more. There would be no war; there would be no poverty; there would be no sadness. The world would be perfect...

VERB	INFINITIVE	SPANISH	TENSE	PERSON
1.				
2.				
3.				
4.				
5.				
6.				
7.				
8.				
9.				
10.				
11.				
12.				
13.				
14.				
15.				
16.				
17.				
18.				
19.				
20.				
21.				
22.				
23.				

PRACTICE E: Translate the text into Spanish.

12. FUTURE/CONDITIONAL CONVERSATION PRACTICE

PRACTICE A: Translate the questions into Spanish and answer in Spanish

1. What will you do this Christmas?
2. Where will you go next weekend?
3. Who will you speak to tomorrow?
4. What would you buy with ten thousand euros?
5. How will you practice Spanish after this course?
6. Would you change anything in your life?
7. How long would you wait in a queue?
8. Will you be in Spain in two years' time?
9. What, if anything, would you change about yourself?
10. Would it be better for the Spanish economy to leave the euro?
11. What will the weather be like in the summer?
12. Where will you go on holiday next year?
13. Where would you like to visit in Spain?
14. Which famous person would you most like to spend a day with?
15. Which job wouldn´t you do?
16. What will you cook on Sunday?
17. What would be your perfect present?
18. Will you speak Spanish tonight?
19. When would you need an interpreter?
20. What would you choose in an Indian restaurant?

12. "SER" AND "ESTAR" - FUTURE/ CONDITIONAL.

WILL BE		WOULD BE	
SER	ESTAR	SER	ESTAR
seré	estaré	sería	estaría
serás	estarás	serías	estarías
será	estará	sería	estaría
seremos	estaremos	seríamos	estaríamos
seréis	estaréis	seríais	estaríais
serán	estarán	serían	estarían

PRACTICE A: Translate using "ser" or "estar". (See "Top Tip" number 5 page 19 for when to use "ser" and when to use "estar").

1. He will be there at 5.
2. They will be very tall in 5 years.
3. I would be happy, but I have no money.
4. She would be a nurse but she doesn't like blood.
5. They will be very angry.
6. You(s) would be there, but there are no more places.
7. We will be at the hotel on Saturday.
8. Barcelona would be a lovely city to visit.
9. Will you be at home tonight?
10. How much would it be for 2 adults and 2 children?

PRACTICE B: Translate using "ser" or "estar".

1. Will you be in Seville for Easter?
2. I think it will be a good match tomorrow.
3. We will be the first in the queue.
4. It would be a very good price, but it doesn't work.
5. He wouldn't be here, but I called him yesterday to invite him.
6. He will be very nice.
7. Will you(s) be happy with the small car?
8. They would be so rich, but they lost all their money at the casino.
9. That would be great.
10. She will be the first female President of the United States.

13. DEMONSTRATIVE ADJECTIVES AND PRONOUNS.

	ADJECTIVES		PRONOUNS		
	Masc.	Fem.	Masc	Fem	Neuter
this	este	esta	éste	ésta	esto
these	estos	estas	éstos	éstas	éstos
that	ese	esa	ése	ésa	eso
those	esos	esas	ésos	ésas	ésos
that over there	aquel	aquella	aquél	aquélla	aquéllo
those over there	aquellos	aquellas	aquéllos	aquéllas	aquéllos

As you see, the demonstrative adjective and pronouns are practically identical, differing only in that the demonstrative pronouns take an accent mark, The demonstrative pronouns replace demonstrative adjectives and take gender and number when this is significant to something in particular. There are no neuter adjectives because as soon as we are describing something in particular, that means that we know its gender.

E.g
This house is mine, but that one is his.- **Esta** casa es mía, pero **ésa** es suya.

These windows are clean but those over there are dirty.- **Estas** ventanas están limpias pero **aquéllas** están sucias.

That chair is comfortable, but this one is uncomfortable.- **Esa** silla es cómoda, pero **ésta** es incómoda.

This table is free, but that one over there was occupied.- **Esta** mesa está libre, pero **aquélla** estaba ocupada.

That car was cheap but this one is expensive.- **Ese** coche era barato pero **éste** es caro.

PRACTICE A: Translate.

1. This book is mine, but that one is his.
2. That house over there is pretty, but this one is prettier.
3. These shoes were mine, and those were his.
4. That boy over there used to be my neighbour, and this one is his friend.
5. That woman is my colleague, but those over there used to work in the office next door.
6. These books are in Spanish but those are in English.
7. That telephone over there didn´t work yesterday but this one did.
8. That dog was in the park last night but that one wasn´t.
9. That car has always worked well but this one has never started.
10. That man over there is French but this one is German.

Neuter Demonstrative Pronouns.

Whenever you are referring to something non-specific (e.g That´s not true) or when you don´t or can´t know the name and therefore the gender (e.g. What is this?), You need to use the neuter demonstrative pronoun.

For this reason, they are normally used in exclamations, questions, and abstractions:

¡Esto es ridiculo!-This is ridiculous
¿Qué es esto?- What is this?
¡Aquello es una monstrosidad!- That is a monstrosity!

PRACTICE B: Translate.

1. This is great
2. What is that?
3. I never do that.
4. Did you do this?
5. That was terrible.
6. This is why I don´t smoke.
7. That is why relationships are so difficult.
8. Who said that?
9. When did I say that?
10. Who wanted that?

14. INDIRECT OBJECT PRONOUNS.

What is an Indirect Object Pronoun? (IOP)

IOPs work in a similar way as **DOP´s**, but whereas the **DOPs** are who or what the action is done to in a sentence, the **IOP** could be described as the DESTINATION where the **DOP** is going. For example, lets take the sentence: **He gives the book to me....**
The direct object is the book as that is **what** he is actually giving, but the indirect object is "me", the person he is giving the book **to**.
Here are the **IOP´s** in Spanish next to their English equivalent. Note that they are very similar to **DOPs** and in fact only vary in the **3rd person singular and plural**:

Direct Object Pronouns		Indirect Object Pronouns	
ENGLISH	SPANISH	ENGLISH	SPANISH
me	me	me	me
you	te	you	te
him/her/it	lo/la	him/her/it	le
us	nos	us	nos
you(s)	os	you(s)	os
them	los/las	them	les

NB: If a sentence has an indirect object, there <u>must</u> be a direct object, although this is sometimes implied rather than stated.

Placement of IOP´s: Just like **DOPs**, an **IOP** goes immediately in front of the conjugated verb, or at the end of Present Participles or infinitives.
E.g. He is writing it to me- "**Me lo** está escribiendo" or "Está escribiendo**melo**."
E.g. I want to tell it to you- "**Te lo** quiero dar" or "Quiero dár**telo**."
In sentences with both a **DOP** and an **IOP** the **IOP** goes first, and if both pronouns begin with the letter **"l"**, the **IOP** converts to **"se"**.
E.g. I said it to him- "**Se lo** dije."
They bought them for her- "**Se las** compraron".
I sang it for him- "**Se lo** canté."
We did it for them- "**Se lo** hicimos."

PRACTICE A: Translate.

1. She told me it yesterday.
2. We didn´t used to buy ourselves them often.
3. They didn´t send it to us.
4. We don´t make it for her every day.
5. He paid you for it in cash.
6. She is going to send it to me tomorrow.
7. I sang it for him.
8. We had to sell it to them.
9. You can send it to me by email.
10. You must buy it for yourself.
11. He didn´t need to pay us for it the day before yesterday.
12. Why do you give it (fem) to me?
13. She is preparing it for herself.
14. He used to buy them for himself.
15. I am keeping them for you.

PRACTICE B: Pick out the 36 verbs in the text below and use them to complete the verb identification table as per the example.

Once I *had* a new neighbour. He lived next door to me. He always seemed (to me) to be very nice. I wanted to give him something nice. I made a cake for him and wrote him a note that said "welcome to the street". I took it over to his house and left it outside his door. The next day he called me by telephone and thanked me for the cake. He gave me some flowers, and I put them in a vase on the table in the living room. They were very pretty.

I now see him every day and at the weekends I make him a cake and we eat it together. Every Sunday he buys flowers for me and he brings them to me, I put them in a vase and take it into the living room. He says that he gives me them because when I made him that cake, I improved his life. I want to improve it for him forever. It was a good day for me when he came to live on my street. He gave me a ring yesterday and he bought it for me in a very expensive shop. I will wear it always and in the summer, we will get married.

VERB	INFINITIVE	SPANISH	TENSE	PERSON
1, I had	To have	tener	preterite	1st p.sing.
2.				
3.				
4.				
5.				

6.				
7.				
8.				
9.				
10.				
11.				
12.				
13.				
14.				
15.				
16.				
17.				
18.				
19.				
20.				
21.				
22.				
23.				
24.				
25.				
26.				
27.				
28.				
29.				
30.				
31.				
32.				
33.				
34.				
35.				
36.				

PRACTICE C: Translate the text into Spanish.

15. POSSESIVE ADJECTIVES AND PRONO

ADJECTIVES- DESCRIBE the noun

Singular	Plural	English
mi	mis	*my*
tu	tus	*your (singular)*
su	sus	*His, her, it´s, their.*
nuestro/a	nuestros/as	*our*
vuestro/a	vuestros/as	*your (plural)*

PRONOUNS- REPLACE the noun

Singular	Plural	English
mío/a	míos/as	*mine*
tuyo/a	tuyos/as	*yours (singular)*
suyo/a	suyos/as	*his, hers, its, theirs*
nuestro/a	nuestros/as	*ours*
vuestro/a	vuestros/as	*yours (plural)*

PRACTICE A: Translate

1, It´s my telephone. It´s mine.
2. It was your food. It was yours.
3. He was her husband. He was hers.
4. They have been our neighbours. They have been ours.
5. They are their tables. They are theirs.
6. They were your (pl) dogs. They were yours.
7. They have been my friends. They have been mine.
8. He was his lawyer. He was his.
9. We were their doctors. We were theirs.
10. They have been your problems. They have been yours.
11. A friend of mine works here.

12. Some friends of his lived there.
13. A colleague of ours had a house in Spain.
14. They have never spoken to him again because he is an enemy of theirs.
15. That restaurant has always been a favourite of mine.

PRACTICE B: Translate

I was very upset because Sarah had my bag. She said it was hers. But I know it was mine because it has my initials. Sarah steals everything. Nothing in her house is hers. Many things are mine. For example all her shoes are mine, the silver ring on her finger is mine, 3 of her scarves and her gloves are mine, even some of the food in the cupboards is mine. What can I do? The law says that possession is 99 percent of the law. Therefore, everything is hers.

36. VERB TABLES- REVISION OF TENSES.

PRACTICE A: Try to complete these verbs tables without looking first of all to see what you can remember so far. It is a good idea to complete in pencil!! Then you can correct if necessary and then come back to re-do the excercise to make sure you can still remember. Repetition is the best way to make things stick!!

1. HABLAR- to speak

PRESENT	P.PERFECT	PRETERITE	IMPERFECT	FUTURE	FUT.COND.

2. PONER- to

PRESENT	P.PERFECT	PRETERITE	IMPERFECT	FUTURE	FUT.COND.

3. ESTAR- to

PRESENT	P.PERFECT	PRETERITE	IMPERFECT	FUTURE	FUT.COND.

4. SER- to

PRESENT	P.PERFECT	PRETERITE	IMPERFECT	FUTURE	FUT.COND.

5. LEER- to

PRESENT	P.PERFECT	PRETERITE	IMPERFECT	FUTURE	FUT.COND.

6. SUBIR- to

PRESENT	P.PERFECT	PRETERITE	IMPERFECT	FUTURE	FUT.COND.

7. VOLVER- to

PRESENT	P.PERFECT	PRETERITE	IMPEERFECT	FUTURE	FUT.COND.

8. IR- to

PRESENT	P.PERFCT	PRETERITE	IMPERFECT	FUTURE	FUT.COND.

9. CANTAR- to

PRESENT	P.PERFECT	PRETERITE	IMPERFECT	FUTURE	FUT.COND.

BREAK THE LANGUAGE BARRIER LEVEL 3

10. QUERER- to

PRESENT	P.PERFECT	PRETERITE	IMPERFECT	FUTURE	FUT.COND.

11. PODER- to

PRESENT	P.PERFECT	PRETERITE	IMPERFECT	FUTURE	FUT.COND.

8. DESPERTARSE- to

PRESENT	P.PERFECT	PRETERITE	IMPERFECT	FUTURE	FUT.COND.

9. ESCRIBIR- to

PRESENT	P.PERFECT	PRETERITE	IMPERFECT	FUTURE	FUT.COND.

10. ACOSTARSE- to

PRESENT	P.PERFECT	PRETRITE	IMPRFECT	FUTURE	FUT.COND.

BREAK THE LANGUAGE BARRIER LEVEL 3

11. VENIR- to

PRESENT	P.PERFECT	PRETERITE	IMPERFECT	FUTURE	FUT.COND.

12. DECIR- to

PRESENT	P.PERFECT	PRETERITE	IMPERFECT	FUTURE	FUT.COND.

13. PENSAR- to

PRESENT	P.PERFECT	PRETERITE	IMPERFECT	FUTURE	FUT.COND.

14. TENER- to

PRESENT	P.PERFECT	PRETERITE	IMPERFECT	FUTURE	FUT.COND.

15. MIRAR- to

PRESENT	P.PERFECT	PRETERITE	IMPERFECT	FUTURE	FUT.COND.

16. COGER - to

PRESENT	P.PERFECT	PRETERITE	IMPERFECT	FUTURE	FUT.COND.

17. CEPILLARSE - to

PRESENT	P.PERFECT	PRETERITE	IMPERFECT	FUTURE	FUT.COND.

18. ANDAR - to

PRESENT	P.PERFECT	PRETERITE	IMPERFECT	FUTURE	FUT.COND.

19. COMPARTIR - to

PRESENT	P.PERFECT	PRETERITE	IMPERFECT	FUTURE	FUT.COND.

20. JUGAR - to

PRESENT	P.PERFECT	PRETERITE	IMPERFECT	FUTURE	FUT.COND.

17. "PARA" OR "POR"? PART I- "PARA".

Para is used in the following circumstances:

a. Destination (where something or someone is going to end up):
E.g. Esta mesa será **para** el salón- This table will be for the living room.

b. The recipient of an action:
E.g. Este regalo es **para** Juan- This present is for Juan.

c. Direction and/or FINAL travel destination:
E.g. El tren salió **para** Madrid a las 9.00- The train left for Madrid at 9.

d. Aim, purpose or objective of actions (plus infinitive) "in order to":
E.g. Carlos estudiaba mucho **para** tener buenas notas - Carlos studied hard to get good marks.

e. Time limits or deadlines in the future:
E.g. Necesito el dinero **para** lunes- I need the money for Monday.

f. Comparison to a certain standard:
E.g. Era alto **para** su edad- He was tall for his age.

g. Opinion or personal standard:
E.g. **Para** mí, aprender español es muy importante- For me (in my opinion), learning Spanish is very important.

PRACTICE A: Translate these sentences into English and say which of the previous criteria is the reason for using "para".

1. Tenéis que pagar la factura para el 31 de Agosto.
2. Carlos tuvo un anillo para ella.
3. Enciendo la tele para ver las noticias.
4. Este verano vamos para Inglaterra.
5. Para él, Maria era la chica más bonita de la clase.
6. Hay que trabajar mucho para recibir buenas notas.
7. Ana asistía a clases para cantar.
8. Esta crema sería para la cara y esa sería para las manos.
9. Este café es barato para un bar en la playa.
10. Este papel es para envolver regalos.
11. Para nosotros, ir al cine los sábados es estupendo.
12. Ellos estudiaban para profesores.
13. Había mucha lluvia para primavera.

14. Para mí, el calor es mejor que el frio.
15. Deberías comprar flores para tu novia el día 14 de Febrero.
16. Esto es para lavar la ropa.
17. Tengo trabajo para el año que viene.
18. Salimos para la oficina a las 9.
19. Esta silla será para el patio.
20. José es muy inteligente para un niño de 11 años.

PRACTICE B: Translate into Spanish (using "para" only).
Say which of the previous criteria is the reason for using "para".

1. This house is perfect for us.
2. We needed a new table for the dining room.
3. It is not important to have a car for some people.
4. These shoes will be for walking in the country.
5. They have to read the book by Thursday.
6. He went to the bar to forget his problems.
7. They left for America yesterday.
8. Are you studying to be an accountant?
9. He was very polite for a teenager.
10. Will you be able to write the letter for Tuesday?
11. This meat is for the dogs.
12. For me, I prefer the red car, but for him, he prefers the black.
13. She worked on Sundays in order to earn more money.
14. What time do you leave for work?

 Top Tips!!

6. "También" or "Tampoco".
Most of you will recognise "también" easily enough as meaning "also" or "too", but do you use the negative "tampoco" when neccessary for "either" or "neither"? E.g:
A mí, me gustan los coches. Yo también.- I like cars. Me too.
No me gustan los perros grandes. Yo tampoco.- I don´t like big dogs. Me neither.
Carmen y Ana nunca trabajan los domingos. Nunca trabajan los días de fiesta tampoco.- Carmen and Ana never work Sundays. They never work bank holidays either.

18. "PARA" OR "POR"? PART II- "POR".

"POR" is used in the following circumstances:

a. Expresses duration of time:
E.g. Vamos de vacaciones por 2 semanas- We are going on holiday for 4 weeks.

b. Indicates periods of time during the 24 hour day, where in English we say "in the morning" or "at night" etc:
E.g. Estudiaba español los martes por la mañana- I used to study Spanish on Tuesday mornings.

c. To say "per":
E.g. Tengo clase de español 3 veces por semana- I have a Spanish class 3 times per week.

d. Indicates an exchange or trade:
E.g Daré 1,000 euros por el coche- I will give 1,000 euros for the car.

e. Expresses substitution (on behalf of or in place of):
E.g. Hablaré por Juan en la reunion- I will speak for Juan at the meeting.

f. Expresses thanks and gratitude:
E.g. Muchas gracias por las flores- Many thanks for the flowers.

g. "Because of":
E.g. No trabajó ayer por estar enfermo- He/she didn´t work yesterday because of being ill.

h. Expresses why someone or something is a certain way:
E.g. Paco era popular por su personalidad- Paco was popular because of his personality.

i. Means of transportation:
E.g. Iremos a Inglaterra por avion- We will go to England by plane.

j. Expresses means of sending messages or information:
E.g. ¿Me escribiste por email? - Did you write to me by email?

k. Indicates a TEMPORARY stop (remember, for FINAL destination use "para"):
E.g. Pasaremos por tu casa cuando vamos para Torrevieja- We will stop by your house when we go to Torrevieja.

l. Indicates movement in an area:
E.g. Pasearán por el parque - They will go for a walk in the park.

m. Expresses an emotion for something or someone:
E.g. Tengo mucho cariño por él - I have a lot of affection for him.

n. Idiomatic expressions:
E.g. **por allí** - over there; **por aqui**- over here; **por ejemplo**- for example; **por eso**- for that reason; **por favor**- please; **por fin**- at last; **por lo general**- normally; **por lo menos**- at least; **por primera vez**- for the first time; **por separado**- separately; **por supuesto**- of course; **por todas partes**- everywhere; **por todos lados**- on all sides.

PRACTICE A: Translate these sentences into English and say which of the previous criteria is the reason for using "por".

1. Ella corría por media hora cada día.
2. Fuimos a Amsterdam por avion.
3. Paseamos por el Centro Comercial pero no compramos nada.
4. Pagamos doscientos euros por el sofá.
5. El coche va a sesenta millas por hora.
6. Busqué el gato por todas partes sin encontrarlo.
7. No tengo ningún sentimiento por tí.
8. Ella siempre trabajaba por la tarde.
9. Gracias por tu ayuda.
10. Siempre recibe buenas notas por estudiar mucho.
11. Tengo tos, ¿puedes hablar por mí?
12. Fui por el supermercado antes de ir al cine.
13. Vamos al teatro el sábado por la noche.
14. No querré pagar más de quince euros por un menú del día
15. Siempre compran comida por separados.
16. Conducíamos por el campo los domingos.
17. Puedes mandarme la información por fax.
18. Nadie trabaja por mí cuando estoy enfermo.
19. Elton John es famoso por sus canciones.
20. Ahora está sin blanco por comprar tantas cosas.

PRACTICE B: Translate these sentences into English and say which of the previous criteria is the reason for using "por".

1. We went to school by bus.
2. You can have those shoes for ten euros.
3. He had at least twenty cats.
4. I will always walk through the park in the morning.
5. We read the papers for an hour every morning.
6. Can you work for Maria today, she is ill.
7. I am going to the supermarket for milk, bread and eggs.
8. He watched the football every Wednesday night.
9. She cannot touch the cat because of her allergies.
10. Thanks for nothing.
11. She deserved a medal for giving so much to others.
12. Ninety per cent of dentists will recommend this toothpaste.
13. He passes by my house once in a while.
14. I have a lot of affection for him.

Top Tips!!

7. PESKY PRONOUNS- A SUMMARY.

SUBJECT PRONOUNS: yo, tú, él/ella, nosotros/as, vosotros/as, ellos/ellas- I, you, he/she/it, we, you(s), they.
E.g. **Yo** soy profesora- **I** am a teacher
POSSESSIVE PRONOUNS: mi/s, tu/s, su/s, nuestro/a/s, vuestro/a/s, su/s- my, your, his/her/its, our, your (plural), their.
E.g. ¿Son **vuestros** hijos? -Are they **your (plural)** children?
REFLEXIVE PRONOUNS: me, te, se, nos, os, se- myself, yourself, him/her/itself, ourselves, yourselves, themselves.
E.g. **Te** duchabas cada día- You had a shower (showered yourself) every day.
DIRECT OBJECT PRONOUNS: me, te, lo/ la, nos, os, los/las- me, you, him/her, us, you(s), them.
E.g. **Nos** invitaron ayer- They invited **us** yesterday.
"PARA"/ "POR" PRONOUNS: mí, ti, él/ella, nosotros/as, vosotros/as, ellos/ellas- me, you, him/her/it, us, you(s), them.
E.g. El coche será para **tí**- the car will be for **you**.
INDIRECT OBJECT PRONOUNS: me, te, le, nos, os, les- me, you, him/her/it, us, you(s), them. Also "se"- used when two "l" pronouns together.
E.g. **Se lo** compraría- I would buy **it** for **him/her**.

14. "PARA" OR "POR"?- COMPARISON A.

PRACTICE A: Translate the sentences below into Spanish using "para" or "por". Give the reason for your choice. Pay attention to the verb tenses.

1. I had a few things for him.
2. Juan is very nice for such a good-looking man.
3. Thank you very much for the chocolates.
4. I like to walk around all the shops in a town.
5. The concert will start at nine o´clock, we want to arrive for eight thirty.
6. I do not like these shoes. They are for teenagers.
7. I always have tea in the morning, but I have coffee in the afternoon. In the evening, I have wine.
8. Those pictures were for the main bedroom.
9. I always go to England by plane, I never go by car.
10. It is a very expensive shop. One hundred euros for a pair of shoes!!
11. Are you ready? We are leaving for the party now.
12. Are you hungry? Is there a restaurant around here?
13. There was no school yesterday because of the snow.
14. Carlos is ill today. Can you work for him?
15. We must do exercise at least three times a week.
16. Maria preferred the summer, but for me, the winter is better.
17. I feel nothing for him.
18. I will contact all my friends by email.
19. John Carpenter is famous for his films.
20. I spoke to my boyfriend on the telephone every day.

 Top Tips!!

8. "En"- "On", "in" or "at".

"En" is a very useful little preposition meaning "on", "in" or "at".
It is much more common in Spanish to say "in" a place rather than "at" a place.

E.g: I will be **at** the beach tomorrow- Estaré **en** la playa mañana.
They were dancing **on** the table- Bailaban **en** la mesa.
They put the table **in** the kitchen- Pusieron la mesa **en** la cocina.

15. "PARA" OR "POR"? - COMPARISON B.

PRACTICE A: Translate into Spanish using the appropriate form of "para" or "por".
Each highlighted word needs one or the other in Spanish although this may not be apparent in English. Pay attention to the tenses of the verbs also, it is always a good idea to identify the verbs before starting the translation.

Yesterday my brother came to my house. He said to me:

"I have an interesting story **for** you. I had a friend who lived in Alicante. He worked **for** a very small company and **for** very little money. He always needed more money **for** food and bills. So every Friday when he bought cigarettes he paid four euros extra **for** two lottery tickets. He chose the numbers **by** birthdays of his friends and family. He did this every week **for** over fifteen years and he never won anything.

During this period, he got married. His parents gave them the money **for** the wedding and he always wanted to thank them properly **for** that. A year later, they had their first child and their second one two years afterwards. They never had enough money **to** buy everything that they needed and there were many things that his children couldn´t have.

Last week, **for the first time**, he won. He won over one million euros. He now has enough money **to** buy everything he wants **for** him, his friends and his family. They are all very grateful **for** these things. Normally, he wouldn´t pay more than two thousand euros **for** a car, but now **because of** winning the lottery, tomorrow he is going to buy a new car **for** fifty thousand euros. Sister, I am very happy **for** him."

The Royal Palace, Madrid.

21. "PARA" OR "POR"? - COMPARISON C.

PRACTICE A: Translate the sentences below into Spanish using "para" or "por". Give the reason for your choice. Pay attention to the verb tenses.

1. For an old man, he has very young ideas.
2. I´m going to send this letter by airmail.
3. He couldn´t come. I had to do the presentation for him.
4. At last, after a long wait, we left the airport.
5. I need to buy a car. I will give you a thousand euros for yours.
6. Spain is known for it´s very interesting history.
7. I had to take medicine 4 times a day.
8. My father works for a large company in Germany.
9. I have no champagne glasses.
10. We learnt Spanish to speak to more people.
11. Normally, I don´t do much on Saturday mornings.
12. Yesterday the weather was terrible. Because of this we decided to stay at home.
13. They called me to invite me to their wedding.
14. She and Pepe are very happy because at last they are going to get married.
15. And because of this, they are going to invite everyone to their wedding.
16. They will have a big party to celebrate.
17. After the wedding, they are both going to leave for Spain.
18. Luisa was born in America, but for an American she speaks Spanish quite well.
19. Tomorrow I will thank them for inviting us to the party.
20. Last week they gave a party to celebrate their engagement.
21. Amy, John and I decided to each give them 50 euros to be able to buy them a nice present.
22. On Saturday we will go to the Shopping Centre to choose something.

BREAK THE LANGUAGE BARRIER LEVEL 3
WWW.ELPRINCIPECENTRE.COM
info@elprincipecentre.org

22. TRANSLATION ENGLISH TO SPANISH MIXED TENSES.

PRACTICE A: Pick out the 41 verbs in this text and use them to complete the verb identification table below as per the example.

Pedro used to stay with his friend Carlos in the summer holidays in the countryside. They would often go to a nearby lake to fish. Generally, they would catch four or five fish but they will never forget what happened to them yesterday when they didn´t catch anything.

It was a lovely day, so they decided to spend the whole day there. They took their fishing rods, 2 chairs, an umbrella, and a cool box with some beers, water and sandwiches. They also took Carlos´ two dogs, Pepe and Pepa, with them. When they arrived at the lake they put their things down on the ground beside the lake and started to fish. They could see many big fish in the lake but an hour went by and nothing happened.

Suddenly, Pedro got up shouting- "I have something, I have something!!". Carlos went to help him, tripped over one of the dogs who were sitting at his feet, and fell into the water. Luckily, he was a good swimmer and he managed to get out of the water without much difficulty.

"You´ll have to dry your clothes", said Pedro.
"If not, you will catch cold".
The two men went home without catching anything. Carlos changed his clothes and they ate their sandwiches and drank their beer on Carlos´ patio.

VERB	INFINITIVE	SPANISH	TENSE	PERSON
1. used to stay	To stay	quedarse	imperfect	3rd p.sing.
2.				
3.				
4.				
5.				
6.				
7.				
8.				
9.				

Copyright 1999-2020© Vicki Marie Riley. All rights reserved.

10.				
11.				
12.				
13.				
14.				
15.				
16.				
17.				
18.				
19.				
20.				
21.				
22.				
23.				
24.				
25.				
26.				
27.				
28.				
29.				
30.				
31.				
32.				
33.				
34.				
35.				
36.				
37.				
38.				
39.				
40.				
41.				

PRACTICE B: Translate into Spanish.

PRACTICE C: Translate and answer these questions in Spanish.

1. Who did Pedro used to stay with in the summer holidays?
2. Where did they often go to fish?
3. How many fish did they normally catch?
4. What will they never forget?
5. What did they take with them apart from their fishing rods and why?
6. Who also went with them?
7. What did they do when they arrived at the lake?
8. What could they see in the lake?
9. What did Pedro do suddenly?
10. What was he shouting?
11. What happened when Carlos went to help him?
12. Did he have problems getting out of the water?
13. Why did Pedro say he'll have to dry his clothes?
14. Where did they eat their sandwiches and drink their drinks?

 Top Tips!!

9. SOME USEFUL SHORTENED WORDS.

Just as in English, some common everyday words are shortened in Spanish in everyday use. Here are a few of them:

1. La película- film- **peli**.
2. El colegio- school- **coli**.
3. El bolígrafo- pen- **boli**.
4. Las patatas- potatos- **papas**.
5. La bicicleta- bicycle- **bici**.
6. El cumpleaños-birthday-**cumpli**.
7. El profesor- teacher- **profe**.
8. Por favor- please- **por fa**.
9. La televisión- television- **tele**.
10. La motocicleta- motorbike- **moto**.

23. THE IMPERATIVE OR COMMAND MODE 1- "TÚ"- SINGULAR INFORMAL.

The imperative only deals with one time frame, which is **NOW**. The person it is directed at is always **YOU**. It is direct, and often contains only one word:

LOOK! LISTEN! STOP! WAIT! SING! DANCE!

As throughout my books, I will only be looking at the informal forms, singular and plural.

Positive commands: Drop the "s" from the **2nd person singular** of the **present simple tense** of the particular verb. **E.g**:
- You speak- **hablas**- speak!- **¡habla!**
- You eat- **comes**- eat!- **¡come!**
- You live- **vives**- live!- **¡vive!**

PRACTICE A: Translate.

1- Work now!
2- Study today!
3- Buy the car!
4- Wait here!
5- Drink this!
6- Run quickly!
7- Learn everything!
8- Sing for him!
9- Dance on the table!
10- Live for today!
11- Write here!
12- Eat more!
13- Read that!
14- Take the money!

Negative commands: Take the present tense of the verb first person singular (yo) and remove the "o". Then for "ar" verbs add "es", and for "er" and "ir" verbs add "as". **E.g**;
- Don´t speak!- **¡No hables!**
- Don´t eat!- **¡No comas!**
- Don´t write!- **¡No escribas!**

Spelling changes: When preceding an "e", the following changes are invoked-
- "c" becomes "qu"- e.g. **ino toques!**
- "g" becomes "gu"- e.g, **ino juegues!**
- "z" becomes "c"- e.g. **ino empieces!**

PRACTICE B: Translate. (Audio 29)

1. Don´t look at the house!
2. Don´t sing that song!
3. Don´t run in the corridor!
4. Don´t study German, study Spanish!
5. Don´t think so much!
6. Don´t believe everything!
7. Don´t open the door!
8. Don´t read my diary!
9. Don´t dance with him!
10. Don´t wait all night!
11. Don´t pay anything yet!
12. Don´t practice all night!
13. Don´t arrive late!
14. Don´t drink too much!

 Top Tips!!

10. SOME HANDY "SLANG" VERBS/ EXPRESSIONS.

1. Picar- to have a snack.
2. Ir/salir de marcha- to go out and have a good time.
3. Pasarlo bomba/en grande/pipa- to have a great time.
4. No tener huevos/cojones- to not have the balls.
5. Estar loca de contento- to be over the moon.
6. Estar cortado/a- to be embarrassed.
7. Dar la paliza (a alguien)- to annoy someone or beat them up.
8. Ser un pesado- to be a pain.
9. Cabrearse- to get annoyed.
10. Tocar las narices/los huevos- to get on someones nerves.
11. Poner los cuernos (a alguien)- to cheat on someone.
12. Estar pachucho- to be ill.

24. IMPERATIVE "TÚ"- IRREGULAR VERBS.

There are not many irregular verbs in the imperative, but below are the most common in their positive and negative forms:

INFINITIVE	POSITIVE	NEGATIVE
Decir: to	dí	no digas
Hacer: to	haz	no hagas
Ir: to	ve	no vayas
Poner: to	pon	no pongas
Salir: to	sal	no salgas
Ser: to	sé	no seas
Tener: to	ten	no tengas
Venir: to	ven	no vengas

PRACTICE A: Find their meanings and use them to translate these sentences.

1. Put the money here!
2. Tell me everything!
3. Make me a cup of tea!
4. Leave the house now!
5. Come to the party early!
6. Be good!
7. Go to the shops!
8. Have the red one!
9. Don´t put the keys there!
10. Don´t say anything!
11. Don´t make the dinner now!
12. Don´t leave this room!
13. Don´t come again!
14. Don´t be silly!
15. Don´t go to school today!
16. Don´t have any more animals!

25. PLACEMENT OF OBJECT PRONOUNS WITH THE IMPERATIVE.

POSITVE- tag on the end.
E.g. dí**melo**, haz**lo**, comprá**selo**, leván**tate**, dá**selo**, pregúnta**selo**.

NEGATIVE- precedes the verb e.g no **me lo** digas, no **se lo** compres, **no lo** hagas.

PRACTICE A: Translate using the appropriate object pronoun. Unless stated otherwise, presume the pronoun is masculine.

1. Buy me it! (f)
2. Give it him!
3. Find me it now!
4. Tell him!
5. Send it them!
6. Write us it! (f)
7. Sell them it!
8. Do me it!
9. Open it for us!
10. Make her it! (f)
11. Don´t touch it
12. Don´t do it for him.
13. Don´t pay them it! (f)
14. Don´t read her it!
15. Don´t close it on me!
16. Don´t make it them! (f)
17. Don´t leave it us!
18. Don´t bring it me!
19. Don´t cook them it!
20. Don´t forget me!

26. THE IMPERATIVE OR COMMAND MODE 2- "VOSOTROS"- PLURAL INFORMAL.

POSITIVE COMMANDS.

Take the infinitive of the verb that you want to use, drop the "r" and add "d" for all verbs except reflexive.

E.g.: Traed! Coged! Hablad! Escribid! Subid! Sed!

Pronouns are again tagged on the end as with "tú" positive commands.

REFLEXIVE VERBS

Do not add a "d" and add the reflexive pronoun to the stem
E.g levántaos!

PRACTICE A: Translate.

1. Go up the stairs!
2. Bring it to me!
3. Brush your teeth
4. Be kind to them!
5. Go to bed!
6. Take it home!
7. Write to them!
8. Wash your hands!
9. Rub it out!
10. Switch it off!
11. Turn it on!
12. Go to sleep!
13. Close the door!
14. Pay the bill!
15. Have a shave!
16. Go!
17. Have it!
18. Have a shower!
19. Be happy!
20. Tell me!

NEGATIVE COMMANDS

"ar" verbs: Take the "o" off the 1st person singular present tense "yo" stem and add **"éis"** –E.g. - **"no trabajéis!"**

"er" and "ir" verbs: Take the "o" off the 1st person singular present tense and add **"áis"** - E.g. - **No comáis! No escribáis!**

There are only 3 irregular verbs:

IR- to go- ¡no vayáis!
SABER- to know- ¡no sepáis!
SER- to be- ¡no seáis!

PRACTICE B: Translate.

1. Don´t go away!
2. Don´t stop yourselves!
3. Don´t repeat yourselves!
4. Don´t bring us anything!
5. Don´t put it there!
6. Don´t hate me!
7. Don´t arrive late!
8. Don´t touch them!
9. Don´t tell him anything!
10. Don´t go yet!
11. Don´t be so mean!
12. Don´t know everything!

 Top Tips!!

11. SOME WORDS WITH DUAL MEANINGS.
1. El camello- The camel or drug pusher.
2. El banco- The bank, bench, or shoal of fish.
3. La caña- Small beer or fishing rod/stair rod.
4. El chorizo- Spicy sausage or swindler.
5. El gato- Cat or car jack.
6. Los vaqueros- Cowboys or jeans.
7. La luna- Moon or car windshield.
8. La yema- Egg yolk or fingertip.
9. El ojo- Eye or keyhole.
10. La estación- The station or season.

27. IMPERATIVE SUMMARY

TÚ- INFORMAL, SINGULAR

POSITIVE: .TAKE THE PRESENT SIMPLE 2ND PERSON SINGULAR FORM, REMOVE THE "S"

NEGATIVE: TAKE THE PRESENT SIMPLE 1ST PERSON SINGULAR, REMOVE THE "O" AND ADD "ES" FOR "AR" VERBS AND "AS" FOR "ER" AND "IR" VERBS.

IRREGULARS: DECIR/DÍ-HACER/HAZ-IR/VE-PONER/PON-SALIR/SAL-SER/SÉ-TENER/TEN-VENIR/VEN

VOSOTROS- INFORMAL, PLURAL

POSITIVE: TAKE THE INFINITIVE, DROP THE "R" AND ADD "D" FOR ALL VERBS EXCEPT REFLEXIVE. FOR REFLEXIVE, DROP THE "R" AND ADD "OS" TO END.

NEGATIVE: "AR" VERBS- TAKE OFF THE "O" FROM THE 1ST PERSON SINGULAR PRESENT TENSE STEM AND ADD "ÉIS". "ER" AND ""IR" VERBS ADD "ÁIS".

IRREGULARS (ONLY 3): IR/ NO VAYÁIS- SABER/ NO SEPÁIS- SER/ NO SEÁIS

28. PRACTICE THE IMPERATIVE.

PRACTICE A: Translate these problems into English

PRACTICE B: Give advice for your friends problems using the imperative. Note that some are singular (tú) and some are plural (vosotros). Give at least one negative example in each.

E.g. **Siempre me levanto tarde**- I always get up late.
 -**Pon la alarma**- Put the alarm on.
 -**Acuéstate más temprano**- Go to bed earlier.
 -**No salgas tanto por la noche**- Don´t go out so much at night.

1. Por la noche no podemos dormir.
2. Últimamente he engordado mucho.
3. Me siento solo a veces.
4. Gastamos mucho dinero y no podemos evitarlo.
5. Mi novio quiere cortar conmigo.
6. No sé que comprar para mi madre para su cumpleaños.
7. No nos gusta nuestro trabajo en la oficina.
8. He perdido mi cartera.
9. No sé que hacer este fin de semana.
10. Estoy resfriada.
11. Nuestro perro es muy agresivo.
12. Quiero aprender español.
13. No queremos vivir más en la ciudad.
14. Me gustaría comprar un nuevo coche.
15. Nuestro hijo es muy travieso.
16. No me gusta el novio de mi amiga.
17. Nunca tengo bastante dinero.
18. Quiero vivir en otro país.
19. Nunca tenemos tiempo para nada.
20. Quiero un coche nuevo pero no muy caro.

29. PRONOUN PRACTICE

PRACTICE A: Complete these boxes with the appropriate pronouns.

SUBJECT PRONOUNS	
ENGLISH	SPANISH

POSSESSIVE PRONOUNS	
ENGLISH	SPANISH

REFLEXIVE PRONOUNS	
ENGLISH	SPANISH

DIRECT OBJECT PRONOUNS	
ENGLISH	SPANISH

INDIRECT OBJECT PRONOUNS	
ENGLISH	SPANISH

"PARA" PRONOUNS	
ENGLISH	SPANISH

PRACTICE B: Translate into Spanish.

1. She gets up every morning at 8 oclock.
2. We went to the Shopping Centre yesterday to buy a present for them.
3. They sold it last week.
4. I have washed my hair three times this week.
5. Do you want to sell your car?
6. The dress in the window is perfect for her.
7. He has a present for you.
8. We went to bed at 11 last night.
9. I saw them yesterday.
10. The day before yesterday he told us the truth.

PRACTICE C: WRITE 6 MORE SENTENCES EACH ONE USING A DIFFERENT TYPE OF PRONOUN.

30. PRACTICE OF PERSONAL PRONOUNS

Example:
The teacher explained the lesson to the students.
The teacher explained it to them.
El profesor explicó la lección a los estudiantes.
El profesor se la explicó.

PRACTICE A: Translate into Spanish

1. He will ask the policeman the address.
   He will ask him it.

2. The grandmother has read her grandaughter a story.
   The grandmother has read it to her.

3. The mother was putting the coat on her son.
   The mother was putting it on him.

4. The salesman had wrapped up the book for us.
   The salesman had wrapped us it up.

5. I asked (made) the teacher a question.
   I asked her it.

6. They always brought flowers for their mother.
   They always bought her them.

7. We recommend this hotel for you(s).
   We recommend it you(s).

8. Will you return the book to me tomorrow?
   Will you return it me tomorrow?

31. SER AND ESTAR MIXED TENSES.

PRACTICE A: CONJUGATE "SER" AND "ESTAR" IN THE TENSES BELOW. TRY TO DO IT FROM MEMORY.

1. PRESENT TENSE

ENGLISH-TO BE	SER	ESTAR

2. PRESENT PERFECT

ENGLISH-TO BE	SER	ESTAR

3. PRETERITE

ENGLISH-TO BE	SER	ESTAR

4. IMPERFECT

ENGLISH-TO BE	SER	ESTAR

5. FUTURE

ENGLISH-TO BE	SER	ESTAR

6. CONDITIONAL.

ENGLISH-TO BE	SER	ESTAR

PRACTICE B: EXPLAIN IN YOUR OWN WORDS WHEN WE USE "SER" AND WHEN WE USE "ESTAR".

PRACTICE C: TRANSLATE THE FOLLOWING USING THE APPROPRIATE VERB AND TENSE.

1. She will be the first female President of the United States.
2. The table is square.
3. They have been teachers for 20 years.
4. They were never in class.
5. They are from Spain.
6. Who is Juan?
7. I have never been his friend.
8. The exam was in the school and it was very difficult.
9. Every week they were more expensive.
10. When is the class?
11. We have been in England.
12. It would be a very good price, but it doesn't work.
13. Are you tired?
14. Are you(s) happy?
15. She is in the garden.

16. They have been ill.
17. I have been very sad.
18. Paris is in France.
19. The children are ill.
20. They will be very tall in 5 years.
21. Where are you from?
22. Where have they been?
23. They were ready to go at 6.
24. The ball is red.
25. Jordi and Maria have been very tired today.
26. How are you?
27. What´s Pedro like?
28. Every Monday the queues were long.
29. On Fridays I was at work until 8 o´clock.
30. The cats have been on the terrace all morning.
31. The house is dirty.
32. José has always been a very good-looking man.
33. Maria and Belén are blonde.
34. Manuel and Begoña have been lawyers in the city since 2005.
35. He has been my best friend for 10 years.
36. When is the Spanish class?
37. The wedding was on Saturday.
38. Are they Spanish?
39. The meal was in a restaurant in the centre of town. It was good.
40. At the wedding, the cutlery that was on the table was silver.
41. David was very intelligent but was never happy with anything..
42. In 1999 I lived in England and I was a student.
43. The last time I was in London I had a terrible experience.
44. I was President of the club for one year.
45. Who was the winner yesterday?
46. It was a terrible party.
47. She was my best friend for ten years.
48. When was the class?
49. How was Miguel yesterday?
50. When I was a child I was always in the park.
51. The coffee in the restaurant yesterday was cold.
52. At 3 o clock I was already at home.
53. Barcelona would be a lovely city to visit.
54. What was Carlos´s father like?
55. Where were you? I was looking for you.

56. She was an actress that I liked very much.
57. Will you be in Seville for Easter?
58. Where is my car?
59. They were always in a good mood and used to tell us funny stories.
60. I was ill and could not go to the party.
61. I wanted to buy the shoes but they were very expensive.
62. Why was he in that car?
63. This apple is brown.
64. When he was in Spain, he was a policeman.
65. Every Monday she was ill and couldn't work.
66. On Fridays the drinks were cheap.
67. He will be there at 5.
68. Every week I was there at his house.
69. Have you(s) ever been students?
70. She was always tall for her age.
71. The shops were always closed on Sundays.
72. They never were very good dancers.
73. You(s) were never here when I needed you/s.
74. I was never strict.
75. They were never in class.
76. Who are we with?
77. Once a month he was happy when she was there.
78. You(s) were often on the beach when I was there.
79. Were you married in 1996?
80. Every year they were open later.
81. You have always been tall.
82. I would be happy, but I have no money.
83. She would be a nurse but she doesn't like blood.
84. They will be very angry.
85. You(s) would be there, but there are no more places.
86. We will be at the hotel on Saturday.
87. My old house was in the centre of town.
88. Will you be at home tonight?
89. How much would it be for 2 adults and 2 children?
90. Juan was very tall and handsome.
91. Every year the holidays were more and more expensive.
92. I think it will be a good match tomorrow.
93. If we go early, we will be first in the queue.
94. Once a month I was a singer in a bar.
95. The table is dirty.

96. He wouldn't be here, but I called him yesterday to invite him.
97. He will be very nice.
98. Will you(s) be happy with the small car?
99. They would be so rich, but they lost all their money at the casino.
100. That would be great.

32. TRANSLATION FROM ENGISH TO SPANISH MIXED TENSES- JUAN PÉREZ´S MEXICAN ADVENTURE.

The life of Juan Pérez, a Spaniard from Salamanca, **_changed_** the day he decided to buy a television in El Corte Inglés. Luck smiled on him with a piece of paper hidden inside that said **"CONGRATULATIONS-YOU HAVE WON A TRIP TO MEXICO FOR 2 PEOPLE"**. Although Juan was single, he didn´t hesitate one moment in accepting the prize. In Mexico he had distant family who still wrote to him and Juan had never left Salamanca in his whole life. One lovely day he got on a plane and went off to Cancún.

When he arrived at the airport, his niece Juanita was waiting for him. Juan had never seen her except in photos. The airport was full of football fans who were enthusiastically greeting the Mexican team, who were returning victorious from a tour of Europe. Between the people, Juan saw a dark and very attractive girl, with raised arms and a sign saying simply **"JUAN"**. As soon as he saw the sign, he approached her.

"I am Juanita", she said, smiling.
"And I am Juan", he replied.

She gave him a kiss on the cheek and he replied with two, as is customary in Spain. They left the airport and got into a yellow car, then drove to the village where Juanita lived. When they arrived, lots of children ran over to the car to look at the stranger, laughing and pointing. Juanita turned off the engine, turned her head to Juan, smiled, and said: "Welcome to Mexico". Juan´s Mexican adventure was beginning...

PRACTICE A: Pick out the 46 verbs in this text and complete the verb identification table below as per the example.

VERB	INFINITIVE	SPANISH	TENSE	PERSON
1. changed	To change	cambiar	preterite	3rd p.sing
2.				
3.				
4.				
5.				
6.				
7.				
8.				
9.				

10.				
11.				
12.				
13.				
14.				
15.				
16.				
17.				
18.				
19.				
20.				
21.				
22.				
23.				
24.				
25.				
26.				
27.				
28.				
29.				
30.				
31.				
32.				
33.				
34.				
35.				
36.				
37.				
38.				
39.				
40.				
41.				
42.				
43.				
44.				
45.				
46.				

PRACTICE B: Translate the text into Spanish.

PRACTICE C: Tranlsate these questions into Spanish and answer in Spanish.

1. What happened when Juan Pérez decided to buy a televisión in El Corte Inglés?
2. Where was he from?
3. What did he find inside?
4. What had he won?
5. Did he hesitate in accepting the prize?
6. Was he married?
7. What did he have in Mexico?
8. What did he do one lovely day?
9. Who was waiting for him at the airport?
10. Had Juan ever seen her?
11. From where were the Mexican team returning?
12. Who did he see between the people?
13. What did he do as soon as he saw the sign?
14. Where did she kiss him?
15. What happened when they arrived in Juanita´s village?
16. What did Juanita say when she turned off the engine and turned her head towards him?

33. QUERIDA PILI

PRACTICE A: Read this text out loud. Pick out the 79 verbs and use them to complete the verb identification table below.

Querida Pili

Tengo que decirte que fue una idea estupenda por parte de mis padres mandarme aquí a Girona a casa de mis tíos. Hicieron bien por que lo estoy pasando muy bien. ¡Claro que no he escrito todavía a mis padres para contárselo! No sé si lo haré aunque, como ves, estoy usando el ordenador de mi tía para escribir unos correos electrónicos.

Me llevo muy bien con mis primos y te juro que hacemos algo interesante todos los días. Aparte de pasarlo bien, también descanso mucho. Me parece que duermo mucho mejor aquí que en casa: quizás tiene algo que ver con el aire, y que ya no fumo. ¿No me crees? Pues, es verdad...

Duermo bien, me levanto bastante tarde y normalmente desayuno y salgo al jardín con un libro y mi Ipod. Allí paso un par de horas leyendo. Mis primos José y María se levantan a las ocho porque los dos tienen exámenes dentro de tres semanas. ¡Pobrecitos!

Te voy a contar unas de las cosas que más me han gustado. El martes pasado fuimos a una barbacoa en un pueblecito cercano. La habían organizado unos amigos de José. Rafael vino con su novia. Compramos la comida y todas las bebidas por la mañana y cargamos el coche de José. ¿Sabes como de viejo es su coche? Bueno, tuvimos un pinchazo en la carretera y estuvimos media hora reparandolo.

Por fin llegamos, preparamos las ensaladas y unas tortillas enormes y empezamos a asar la carne. Después bailamos y charlamos hasta las cuatro de la mañana. No llegamos a casa hasta la madrugada porque José no logró arrancar el coche y mi tío tuvo que venir para recogernos. Con suerte, ¡no se enfadó!

BREAK THE LANGUAGE BARRIER LEVEL 3
WWW.ELPRINCIPECENTRE.COM
info@elprincipecentre.org

El sábado pasado mis tíos me llevaron a ver a un tío mío que no había visto durante casí diez años. Me contaba historias de cuando vivía en Los Estados Unidos y trabajaba para un banco internaciónal. Viajaba por todo el mundo y hacía muchas cosas intersantes. El fin de semana que viene me llevarán mis tíos a un concierto de Estopa, tengo muchas ganas de ir. El concierto estará en Barcelona y nos quedaremos alli 2 noches, ya te contaré todo en mi próximo email.

Bueno, te dejo porque estamos a punto de salir para el mercadillo. Muchos recuerdos a tus padres y a tu hermano

Un abrazo fuerte- Mercedes

VERB	INFINITIVE	ENGLISH	TENSE	PERSON

PRACTICE B: Translate the text into English.

PRACTICE C: Translate these questions into Spanish and reply in Spanish.

1. Who sent Pili to Girona?
2. Is she having a good time?
3. Has she written to her parents yet?
4. Why does she think that she sleeps better there than at home?
5. What does she normally do after she gets up?
6. Why do her cousins get up at 8 o´clock?
7. Where did they go last Tuesday?
8. Who had organized it?
9. What happened on the road?
10. Until what time did they dance and chat?
11. Why didn´t they arrive home until the early hours of the morning?
12. Where did her aunt and uncle take her last Saturday?
13. Where did her uncle used to work?
14. Where will her aunt and uncle take her next Saturday?
15. How long will they stay there?
16. What is she going to do now?

34. PREPOSITIONS- What is a preposition?

A preposition is a word used to show a relationship between a noun or a pronoun in a sentence and another word in the same sentence. They can relate to place, time, direction, manner and many other things. It is impossible to replace them with another word as they are so specific in meaning. How else could you say "with", "to" or "at"?

1. Prepositions that show a relationship between people and/or things:

About- **acerca de**
On, about -**sobre**
According to - **según**
Against- **contra**
Without- **sin**

With- **con**
Instead of- **en vez de, en lugar de**
Except- **excepto, menos, salvo**
Besides, in addition to- **además de**

PRACTICE A: Translate.

1. He was a person without problems.
2. She always used to talk about her boyfriend.
3. I will always speak against violence.
4. According to my best friend, it was the best film he had ever seen.
5. Besides flowers, her husband buys her chocolate every week.
6. We like everything here except the view.
7. They wanted chips with everything.
8. I bought a book on the history of Spain.
9. Can you give me rice instead of pasta please.

2. Prepositions of place:

Sobre- enfrente de- entre- en- detrás de- cerca de- lejos de- delante de- dentro de- al lado de- encima de- fuera de- a la izquierda de- a la derecha de - debajo de

PRACTICE B: Make sure you know what all these mean and then describe the classroom using as many prepositions of place as possible.

BREAK THE LANGUAGE BARRIER LEVEL 3
WWW.ELPRINCIPECENTRE.COM
info@elprincipecentre.org

3. Prepositions of movement:

Along- **a lo largo de**	Around- **alrededor de**
Backward(s)- **hacia atrás**	Beyond- **más allá de**
Forward(s)- **hacia delante**	Sideways- **de lado**
Through, throughout- **por**	Toward(s)- **hacia**

PRACTICE C: Translate.

1. He always ran around the lake every morning.
2. We will walk along the main street up to the post office.
3. The police searched throughout the house.
4. I always have to look forward to the future, not backwards to the past.
5. They drove toward the river then walked along the path.
6. She looked beyond the tree and she could see the house.
7. Crabs walk sideways.
8. I would not go beyond this point.

4. Prepositions of origin and destination:

Origin-	**Destination-**
Because of /for- **A causa de/por**	Towards- **hacia**
By- **por/de**	To- **a**
From/of- **de**	For (purpose/destination)- **para**

PRACTICE D: Translate.

1. I couldn´t go yesterday because of the weather.
2. I have read all of Stephen King´s books.
3. This present is for you.
4. We will go to the concert on Saturday.
5. He didn´t buy the car because of the price.
6. We chose this rug for the living room.
7. These cups are from Japan.
8. The birds would fly towards the sea.

5. Prepositions of time:

After- **después de**
Before- **antes de**
During/for- **durante**
Since- **desde**
Until- **hasta**

Afterwards- **después**
Beforehand- **antes**
In (the morning etc)- **por**
To/until- **a**

PRACTICE E: *Translate.*

1. You don´t have to be here until tomorrow
2. We needed to fix the car before the winter.
3. It has been very hot since the beginning of June.
4. She wanted to believe in life after death.
5. What are you going to do during the summer?
6. They told me the truth beforehand.
7. He normally makes a cup of tea during the adverts.
8. I was in Portugal for nearly two years.
9. We used to work from Monday to Saturday without a break.
10. I will watch the film and have dinner afterwards.

35. CONVERSATION TRANSLATION PALOMA AND JUAN

PRACTICE A: TRANSLATE WHAT PALOMA AND JUAN DID AT THE WEEKEND.

JUAN: On Saturday I got up very late becaused I was exhausted after working so hard during the week.

PALOMA: What do you call late?

JUAN: Half past twelve or one o´clock. It was almost lunch time. My wife wasn´t very pleased because she wanted to go shopping with me in the morning.

PALOMA: So you had to go in the afternoon?

JUAN: Of course. And it was endless, because the shops were crowded. So, when we got back, my wife prepared a quick dinner and we sat down to watch television until half past eleven. What did you do?

PALOMA: I went to a wedding on Saturday. A cousin of mine was getting married.

JUAN: Did you have a good time?

PALOMA: Yes, it was fine. The food was very good and the drink too, of course. There was music and dancing until three in the morning.

JUAN: And Sunday, what did you do?

PALOMA: Nothing important, Sleep, read the paper and watch television. And you?

JUAN: More or less the same as you.

36. EMAILS

PRACTICE A: Write these imaginary emails in Spanish paying attention to the points indicated that you need to mention.

1. Your friend wants to come and visit you in Spain in September. You have a trip back to the UK organised on the 13th for 10 days. He/she wants to come for two weeks but you think that is too long and only want them to come for a week. Make an excuse. They have asked you what are the best restaurants and general things to do around your area. They also want to know what the weather will be like. Tell them. You also want them to bring something with them from their town. Write an email with all theses points.

2. You bought a computer from a local shop 3 months ago and it is not working properly. They have given you the email address for technical support and you have to email them and explain the problem. Tell them you need the computer for work so it must be fixed as soon as possible. Give them your name, address and contact details; tell them when and where you bought it and request that they contact you within 24 hours.

3. Send an email to a prospective employer regarding a job offer in a local paper. Introduce yourself and tell them you are attaching your CV and briefly describe one similar job you have had, Ask for details of working hours, pay, holidays etc, and offer to come in for an interview. Tell them you are available to start work immediately.

4. Write an email to a Spanish School requesting details of classes. Explain your level, what Spanish you have done before, what sort of course you are looking for etc. Explain when you are available for classes and whether you want to join a group or prefer one to one. Ask exactly where the school is situated, is there any parking, and how much the classes cost. Also ask what you need to bring with you, if you need to buy a book, and if explanations are given in English.

37. POSTSCRIPT

I hope you have enjoyed this book and that your Spanish has improved accordingly. Go over the excercises on a regular basis and practise speaking and listening as often as possible. Repetition and practice is essential for fluidity and confidence with your Spanish, but remember not to be too hard on yourself and expect immediate perfection. You will get it wrong many times before you get it right!!

Keep up the practice as much as possible. Listen to Spanish radio, watch the Spanish TV, go to the Spanish cinema and change the language on your Netflix.

When you are confident with all the components of this Level 3 course you should be communicating effectively in Spanish in the past tenses and ready to move on to Level 4.

Don´t forget the YouTube channel, where you will find the audio of all the exercises. The link is below, the videos are numbered and the page numbers are in the description. Please give a thumbs up if you find the video useful, and subcribe for updates (this is FREE, no cost involved).

You will also find all social media links and contact details.

Lastly, if you have the time and feel so inclined, please leave a review on Amazon of this book and how it has helped you to learn Spanish. Thank you ☺

Happy practising!!!

Vicki

Facebook: https://www.facebook.com/elprincipecentre/
Instagram: https://www.instagram.com/elprincipecentre/
Twitter: @PrincipeCentre
YouTube: https://www.youtube.com/channel/UCm38MRBMVXrV6JblhmQ7xOg
Blog: Confessions of a Spanish teacher:
https://confessionsofaspanishteacher.wordpress.com/

BREAK THE LANGUAGE BARRIER LEVEL 3
WWW.ELPRINCIPECENTRE.COM
info@elprincipecentre.org

38. KEY TO "TOP TIPS".

	PAGE NUMBER
1. "IR A" OR "IR DE"?	4
2. "BIEN" OR "BUENO"?	10
3. "GENTE"- PEOPLE.	13
4. "YA".	17
5. "SER" OR "ESTAR"- REMEMBER THE DIFFERENCE?	20
6. "TAMBIÉN" OR "TAMPOCO"?	43
7. PESKY PRONOUNS- A SUMMARY.	46
8. "EN".	47
9. SOME USEFUL SHORTENED WORDS.	52
10. SOME HANDY "SLANG" VERBS/EXPRESSIONS.	54
11. SOME WORDS WITH DUAL MEANINGS.	55

39. ANSWERS.

1. CUÉNTANOS DE TÍ.

PRACTICE A: The answers are free but the correct verb form is given:

1. ¿Dónde vivías antes de venir a España? *Vivía ......*
2. ¿Qué hacías? *Trabajaba en/ Era .....*
3. ¿Trabajas ahora? *Sí, trabajo/ No, no trabajo ...*
4. ¿Cómo es tu pareja? *Es ...*
5. ¿Tienes (algunas) mascotas? *Si, tengo/ No, no tengo ...*
6. ¿Por qué y cuando viniste a España? *Vine ...*
7. ¿Cómo has practicado el español desde tu última clase? *He ...*
8. ¿Qué malas experiencias has tenido en España? *He tenido/ No he tenido ..*
9. ¿Cuánto tiempo has estudiado el español? *He estudiado ...*
10. ¿Fuiste de vacaciones el año pasado? *Sí, fui/ No, no fui ...*
11. ¿Qué consejo tienes para los otros estudiantes para aprender el español bien? *Free answer.*
12. ¿Cuáles/ Qué son los problemas más grandes que has tenido en aprender español? *Free answer.*
13. ¿Qué quieres lograr después de este curso? *Free answer.*
14. ¿Cuándo fue la última vez que hablaste español? *Free answer.*

3. MIXED TENSE CONVERSATION PRACTICE.

PRACTICE A:

1. ¿Qué hiciste anoche?
2. ¿Has hecho algo tonto alguna vez?
3. ¿Has escrito un poema alguna vez?
4. ¿Cuándo eras niño/a, tenías (algunos) animales?
5. ¿Qué querías ser?
6. ¿Adónde fuiste anteayer?
7. ¿Has estudiado alemán alguna vez?
8. ¿Con quién hablaste el sábado?
9. ¿Siempre hacías los deberes en el colegio?

10. ¿Has tenido un accidente alguna vez?
11. ¿Qué te pusiste ayer?
12. ¿Dónde estaba tu primera casa?
13. ¿De qué color era tu primer coche?
14. ¿Cuándo tuviste tu primera clase de español?
15. ¿Por qué viniste a España?
16. ¿A qué hora te acostaste el lunes pasado?
17. ¿Te duchaste ayer?
18. ¿Has tenido un perro alguna vez?
19. ¿Has conocido a alguien famoso alguna vez?
20. ¿A quién viste el fin de semana?
21. ¿Qué fue el último libro que leíste?
22. ¿Has ganado un premio alguna vez?
23. ¿Sabías español antes de venir aqui?
24. Cuándo eras niño/a, ¿sabías nadar?
25. ¿Cuándo ibas de vacaciones?
26. ¿Has perdido todo tu dinero alguna vez?

FREE ANSWERS

4. TRANSLATION AND COMPREHENSION PRACTICE PRESENT AND PAST TENSES.

PRACTICE A:

VERB	INFINITIVE	SPANISH	TENSE	PERSON
1. were sitting	To sit	sentarse	imperfecto	3rd p.plur
2. they were	To be	ser	imperfecto	3rd p.plur
3. they were not wearing	To wear	llevar	imperfecto	3rd p.plur
4. they were	To be	estar	imperfecto	3rd p.plur
5. they had heard	To hear	oir	past perfect	3rd p.plur
6. was going to	To go	ir	imperfecto	3rd p.sing
7. to rob	To rob	robar	infinitive	
8. they were	To be	estar	imperfecto	3rd p.plur
9. it was	To be	ser	imperfecto	3rd p.sing
10. had not opened	To open	abrir	past perfect	3rd p.sing
11. there weren´t		haber	imperfecto	3rd p.sing
12. is it	To be	ser	present	3rd p.sing
13. said	To say	decir	preterite	3rd p.sing

14. that´s	To be	ser	present	3rd p.sing
15. they told	To tell	decir	preterite	3rd p.plur
16. said	To say	decir	preterite	3rd p.sing
17. they´ve told	To tell	decir	pres.perfect	3rd p.plur
18. we must	To "must"	deber	present	1st p.plur
19. wait	To wait	esperar	infinitive	
20. we can	To "can"	poder	present	1st p.plur
21. go	To go	ir	infinitive	
22. they waited	To wait	esperar	preterite	3rd p.plur
23. opened	To open	abrir	preterite	3rd p.sing
24. entered	To enter	entrar	preterite	3rd p.sing
25. parked	To park	aparcar	preterite	3rd p.sing
26. got out	To get out	bajar	preterite	3rd p.plur
27. entered	To enter	entrar	preterite	3rd p.plur
28. I think	To think	pensar	present	1st p.sing
29. it´s	To be	ser	present	3rd p.plur
30. said	To say	decir	preterite	3rd p.sing
31. they called	To call	llamar	preterite	3rd p.plur
32. entered	To enter	entrar	preterite	3rd p.sing
33. had started	To start	empezar	past perfect	3rd p.sing
34. were carrying	To carry	llevar	imperfect	3rd p.plur
35. had made	To make	hacer	past perfect	3rd p.plur
36. lie down	To lie down	tumbarse	infinitive	
37. were putting (in)	To put in	meter	imperfect	3rd p.plur
38. to give	To give	dar	infinitive	
39. arrested	To arrest	detener	preterite	3rd p.sing
40. spoke	To speak	hablar	preterite	3rd p.plur
41. leaving	To leave	salir	infinitive	
42. have done	To do	hacer	pres. perfect	2nd p.plur
43. they told	To tell	decir	preterite	3rd p.plur
44. let´s go	To go	ir	present	1st p.plur
45. we can	To can	poder	present	1st p.plur
46. go	To go	ir	infinitive	

PRACTICE B:

Paco y José se sentaban en un coche fuera del banco en la calle mayor. Eran policía los dos pero no llevaban uniformes y estaban en el coche pequeño y gris de Paco. Habían oido que alguien iba a robar el banco.

Estaban al lado de la acera en el otro lado de la calle. Eran las 8 de la mañana. El banco no había abierto todavía y no había mucha gente en la calle.

"¿Es hoy?" dijo Paco.

"Esto es lo que me dijeron" dijo José. "Siempre me han dicho la verdad. Debemos esperar por lo menos una hora, después podemos ir a casa".

Esperaron hasta las ocho y cuarto. El banco abrió y entró mucha gente. A las ocho y cuarenta y cinco una furgoneta negra aparcó fuera. Dos hombres bajaron de la furgoneta y entraron en el banco.

"Creo que son ellos", dijo Paco, y llamaron para ayuda.

El policía entró en el banco cinco minutos después y el robo ya había empezado. Los hombres llevaban pistolas y habían hecho a todos los clientes tumbarse con las manos detrás de la cabeza. Los cajeros metían el dinero en bolsas para dar a los ladrones. El policía detuvo a los ladrones inmediatamente sin problemas y Paco y José hablaron con ellos antes de salir.

"Habéis hecho bien", les dijeron. "Vamos a la comisaría con ellos ahora y después podemos ir a casa.

PRACTICE C:

1. ¿Dónde se sentaban Paco y José? Se sentaban en un coche fuera del banco en la calle mayor.
2. ¿Qué eran? Eran policía.
3. ¿Llevaban uniformes? No, no llevaban uniformes.
4. ¿En cuál coche estaban? Estaban en el coche pequeño y gris de Paco.
5. ¿Qué habían oído? Habían oído que alguien iba a robar el banco.
6. ¿Donde estaban? Estaban al lado de la acera en el otro lado de la calle.
7. ¿Qué hora era? Eran las ocho de la mañana.
8. ¿Había abierto el banco? No, no había abierto todavía.
9. ¿Había mucha gente en la calle? No, no había mucha gente.
10. ¿Cuánto tiempo deben esperar? Deben esperar por lo menos una hora.
11. ¿Qué pueden hacer entonces? Pueden ir a casa.
12. ¿Hasta qué hora esperaron? Esperaron hasta las ocho y cuarto.
13. ¿Qué pasó cuando abrió el banco? Entró mucha gente.
14. ¿Qué pasó a las nueve menos cuarto? A las ocho y cuarenta y cinco una furgoneta negra aparcó fuera.
15. ¿Qué hicieron los dos hombres? Los dos hombres bajaron de la furgoneta y entraron en el banco.
16. ¿Qué hicieron Paco y José? Llamaron para ayuda.
17. ¿Cuándo entró el policía en el banco? El policía entró en el banco cinco minutes después.

18. ¿Qué había pasado dentro? El robo ya había empezado.
19. ¿Qué llevaban los hombres? Llevaban pistolas.
20. ¿Qué habían hecho hacer a los clientes? Habían hecho a todos los clientes tumbarse con las manos detrás de la cabeza.
21. ¿Qué hacían los cajeros? Los cajeros metían el dinero en bolsas para dar a los ladrones.
22. ¿Qué hizo el policía inmediatamente? El policía detuvo a los ladrones inmediatamente sin problemas.
23. ¿Con quién hablaron Paco y José antes de salir? Hablaron con el policía.
24. ¿Qué hicieron todos entonces? Fueron todos a la comisaría.

5. FUTURE- "GOING TO".

PRACTICE A:

1. ¿Qué vais a hacer en Navidad?
2. Van a visitar Sevilla en Mayo.
3. Luis va a dejar de fumar un día.
4. Voy a decirle la verdad/ Le voy a decir la verdad.
5. Vas a ir a la fiesta?
6. Va a ser muy difícil.
7. No vamos a estar felices.
8. ¿Van a hacer la cena o no?
9. ¿Cuándo vas a a hacerlo?/ ¿Cuándo lo vas a hacer?
10. Van a querer muchas cosas.
11. Carmen va a levantarse/ se va a levantar temprano mañana.
12. No lo voy a comprar/ voy a comprarlo todavía.
13. Mis padres van a estar muy enfadados.
14. No van a estar muy felices.
15. Los perros van a tener mucha hambre luego.

BREAK THE LANGUAGE BARRIER LEVEL 3
WWW.ELPRINCIPECENTRE.COM
info@elprincipecentre.org

PRACTICE B:

VERB	INFINITIVE	SPANISH	TENSE	PERSON
1. is	To be	ser	present	3rd p.sing
2. I am going	To go	ir	"going to"	1st p.sing
3. to have	To have	tener	infinitive	
4. I am going	To go	ir	"going to"	1st p.sing
5. to invite	To invite	invitar	infinitive	
6. I have	To have	tener	present	1st p.sing
7. I have	To have	tener	present	1st p.sing
8. I always do	To do	hacer	present	1st p.sing
9. I normally buy	To buy	comprar	present	1st p.sing
10. I am going	To go	ir	"going to"	1st p.sing
11. to tell	To tell	decir	infinitive	
12. I want	To want	querer	present	1st p.sing
13. he is going	To go	ir	"going to"	3rd p.sing
14. to make	To make	hacer	infinitive	
15. he is going	To go	ir	"going to"	3rd p.sing
16. to deliver	To deliver	entregar	infinitive	
17. are going	To go	ir	"going to"	3rd p.plur
18. to come	To come	venir	infinitive	
19. they are going	To go	ir	"going to"	3rd p.plur
20. to bring	To bring	traer	infinitive	
21. we are going	To go	ir	"going to"	1st p.plur
22. to have	To have	tener	infinitive	
23. is going	To go	ir	"going to"	3rd p.sing
24. to make	To make	hacer	infinitive	
25. we are going	To go	ir	"going to"	1st p.plur
26. to enjoy	To enjoy	disfrutar	infinitive	
27. is going	To go	ir	"going to"	3rd p.sing
28. to be	To be	estar	infinitive	
29. I know	To know	saber	present	1st p.sing
30. she isn´t going	To go	ir	"going to"	3rd p.sing
31. to be	To be	estar	infinitive	
32. planning	To plan	planear	infinitive	

PRACTICE C:

Mañana es el cumpleaños de mi hermana. Voy a tener una fiesta para ella. Voy a invitar a mucha gente/ muchas personas porque tengo una casa grande. Tengo muchas fiestas y siempre hago algo especial. Normalmente
compro una tarta y voy a decir al panadero que quiero muchas flores y el nombre de mi hermana en la tarta. Va a hacer una tarta muy especial para ella y la va a entregar mañana por la mañana. Todos los amigos de mi hermana van a venir a la fiesta y van a traer regalos y flores para ella. Vamos a tener muchos juegos y música, y su novio va a hacer muchos cócteles. Vamos a disfrutarla y mi hermana va a estar muy soprendida y contenta. Sé que no va a estar enfadada conmigo para planearla sin su permiso.

PRACTICE D:

1. ¿Qué día es mañana? Mañana es el cumpleaños de su hermana.
2. ¿Qué va a tener? Va a tener una fiesta para ella.
3. ¿Por qué va a invitar a mucha gente? Va a invitar a mucha gente porque tiene una casa grande.
4. ¿Qué siempre hace? Siempre hace algo especial.
5. ¿Qué compra normalmente? Normalmente compra una tarta.
6. ¿Qué va a decir al panadero? Va a decir al panadero que quiere muchas flores y el nombre de su hermana en la tarta.
7. ¿Qué va a hacer y cuando va a entregarla? Va a hacer una tarta muy especial para ella y la va a entregar mañana por la mañana.
8. ¿Quiénes van a venir a la fiesta? Todos los amigos de su hermana van a venir a la fiesta.
9. ¿Que van a traer? Van a traer regalos y flores para ella.
10. ¿Qué van a tener? Van a tener muchos juegos y música.
11. ¿Qué va a hacer el novio de su hermana? Va a hacer muchos cócteles.
12. ¿Van a disfrutarla? Si, van a disfrutarla.
13. ¿Cómo va a estar su hermana? Va a estar muy soprendida y contenta.
14. ¿Va a estar enfadada para planearla sin su permiso? No, no va a estar enfadada.

6. FUTURE- "WILL".

PRACTICE A:

1. Viviré en mi propia casa pronto.
2. ¿Adónde irás el sábado?

3. No lo llevaré de nuevo/ otra vez.
4. ¿Cuándo lo verá de nuevo?
5. Nunca comprarán una casa.
6. Nunca comeremos más en este restaurante.
7. Hablaré español todo el tiempo en clase
8. Trabajará para un banco en Santander.
9. Disfrutaré mis vacaciones el mes que viene.
10. Se levantará a las seis de la madrugada mañana.
11. Pasaremos todo el día en la playa.
12. Irán al cine el jueves.
13. No la dejará en paz.
14. ¿Cuándo volveréis a Inglaterra?
15. ¿Quedarás en un hotel?
16. Dijeron que irán a la fiesta.
17. No compraré nada en el mercadillo.
18. Me lavaré el pelo esta noche.
19. Estudiarán español tres veces por semana.
20. ¿Te ducharás esta noche o por la mañana?

PRACTICE B:

1. **saber**- to know- sabré, sabrás, sabrá, sabremos, sabréis, sabrán.
2. **venir**- to come- vendré, vendrás, vendrá, vendremos, vendréis, vendrán.
3. **querer**- to want- querré, querrás, querrá, querremos, querréis, querrán.
4. **poner**- to put- pondré, pondrás, pondrá, podremos, pondréis, pondrán.
5. **decir**- to say/tell- diré, dirás, dirá, diremos, diréis, dirán.
6. **haber**- to have/auxiliary- habré, habrás, habrá, habremos, habréis, habrán.
7. **poder**- to be able- podré, podrás, podrá, podremos, podréis, podrán.
8. **salir**- to leave/go out- saldré, saldrás, saldrá, saldremos, saldréis, saldrán.
9. **hacer**- to do/ make- haré, harás, hará, haremos, haréis, harán.
10. **caber**- to fit- cabré, cabrás, cabrá, cabremos, cabréis, cabrán.
11. **valer**- to be worth- valdré, valdrás, valdrá, valdremos, valdréis, valdrán.

PRACTICE C:

1. ¿Cuándo sabréis?
2. Habrán (algunos) refrescos.
3. ¿Qué dirá a ellos?
4. Haré el plan mañana.

5. Tendrán el contracto la semana que viene.
6. Querré una taza de té luego.
7. ¿A qué hora vendrá?
8. ¿Pondrás los juegos en el armario luego?
9. No podremos ir a la fiesta el viernes.
10. ¿Cabrá en ese rincon?
11. Su avión saldrá a las diez.
12. ¿Qué valdrán el año que viene?

PRACTICE D: FREE ANSWERS.

PRACTICE E:

VERB	INFINITIVE	SPANISH	TENSE	PERSON
1. I will leave	To leave	dejar	future	1st p. sing
2. I will go	To go	ir	future	1st p. sing
3. to live	To live	vivir	infinitive	
4. I will sell	To sell	vender	future	1st p. sing
5. I own	To own	poseer	present	1st p. sing
6. I will start	To start	empezar	future	1st p. sing
7. I have saved	To save	ahorrar	p. perfect	1st p. sing
8. to live	To live	vivir	infinitive	
9. I am careful	To have care	Tener cuidado	present	1st p. sing
10. I wont be able	To be able	poder	future	1st p. sing
11. To buy	To buy	comprar	infinitive	
12. I will spend	To spend	pasar	future	1st p. sing
13. we will be able	To be able	poder	future	1st p. plural
14. to travel	To travel	viajar	infinitive	
15. we will vist	To visit	visitar	future	1st p. plural
16. we will meet	To meet	conocer	future	1st p. plural
17. I will get up	To get up	levantarse	future	1st p. sing
18. I will go to bed	To go to bed	acostarse	future	1st p. sing
19. I won´t always have to	To have to	Tener que	future	1st p. sing
20. look at	To look at	mirar	infinitive	
21. I will go	To go	ir	future	1st p. sing
22. I will sit	To sit	sentarse	future	1st p. sing
23. I want	To want	querer	present	1st p. sing

24. I will drink	To drink	beber	future	1st p. sing
25. I won´t have	To have	tener	future	1st p. sing
26. I won´t be able	To be able	poder	future	1st p. sing
27. to buy	To buy	comprar	infinitive	
28. I will be	To be	estar	future	1st p. sing
29. will be	To be	ser	future	3rd p. sing
30. I won´t want	To want	querer	future	1st p. sing

PRACTICE F:

En un par de meses dejaré mi trabajo y iré a vivir en España. Venderé todo que poseo y empezaré una vida nueva. He ahorrado bastante dinero para vivir por diez años si tengo cuidado. No podré comprar muchas cosas pero pasaré más tiempo con mi familia y podremos viajar por España. Visitaremos nuevos lugares y conoceremos a gente nueva.

Me levantaré tarde y me acostaré tarde. No siempre tendré que mirar el reloj. Iré a la playa por el día y me sentaré fuera por la tarde. Cuando quiero, beberé vino. No tendré casa grande ni coche grande, no podré comprar mucha ropa ni cosas caras pero estaré feliz. Por primera vez, mi realidad y mis sueños serán iguales. No querré mucho, solo los placeres sencillos de la vida.

7. FUTURE TENSE IN CONTEXT.

PRACTICE B:

VERB	INFINITIVE	ENGLISH	TENSE	PERSON
1. hay	haber	There are	present simple	3 p.sing.
2. es	ser	To be	present	3 p.sing.
3. salió	salir	To leave	preterite	3 p.sing.
4. hace	hacer	To do/make	present	3 p.sing.
5. ver	ver	To see	infinitive	
6. cuenta	contar	To tell	present	3 p.sing.
7. dice	decir	To say/tell	present	3 p.sing.
8. hace	hacer	To do/make	present	3 p.sing.
9. se divierte	divertirse	To have fun	present	3 p.sing.
10. dice	decir	To say/tell	present	3 p.sing.
11. ha conocido	conocer	To meet/know	p. perfect	3 p.sing.
12. dice	decir	To say/tell	present	3 p.sing.
13. saldrán	salir	To leave/ go out	future	3 p.plural.

14. visitarán	visitar	To visit	future	3 p.plural.
15. me acuerdo	acordarse	To remember	present	1 p. sing.
16. trabajaba	trabajar	To work	imperfect	1 p. sing
17. volverá	volver	To return	future	3 p.sing.
18. creo	creer	To believe	present	1 p. sing.
19. llegará	llegar	To arrive	future	3 p.sing.
20. viene	venir	To come	present	3 p.sing.
21. acompañará	acompañar	To accompany	future	3 p.sing.
22. ha conocido	conocer	To meet/know	p. perfect.	3 p.sing.
23. dice	decir	To say/tell	present	3 p.sing.
24. ha invitado	invitar	To invite	p. perfect.	3 p.sing.
25. sabe	saber	To know	present	3 p.sing.
26. aceptará	aceptar	To accept	future	3 p.sing.
27. cree	creer	To believe	present	3 p.sing.
28. está	estar	To be	present	3 p.sing.
29. conoció	conocer	To meet	preterite	3 p.sing.
30. estar	estar	To be	infinitive	
31. podré	poder	To be able	future	1 p.sing.
32. irme	irse	To go	infinitive	
33. viene	venir	To come	present	3 p.sing.
34. tendré	tener	To have	future	1 p. sing.
35. iré	ir	To go	future	1 p. sing.
36. ver	ver	To see	infinitive	
37. tendré	tener	To have	future	1 p. sing.
38. es	ser	To be	present	3 p.sing.
39. acompañaré	acompañar	To accompany	future	1 p. sing.
40. es	ser	To be	present	3 p.sing.
41. dice	decir	To say/tell	present	3 p.sing.
42. dará	dar	To give	future	3 p.sing.
43. invito	invitar	To invite	present	1 p. sing.
44. vamos	ir	To go	present	1 p. plur.
45. celebrar	celebrar	To celebrate	infinitive	
46. parece	parece	To seem	present	3 p.sing.
47. tomar	tomar	To take	infinitive	

PRACTICE C:

PEDRO: Hello Juan. There are two emails in the computer for you.
JUAN: Ah, this one is from José. He left on holiday to England five days ago. Let´s see what he says... He says it is very cold but he is having a lot of fun. He also says that he has met a really nice English girl. He says that tomorrow they will leave for the North and that they will visit some country villages together.
PEDRO: Ah, I remember when I used to work with José at the bank. When will he come back?
JUAN: I think he will arrive in Barcelona next week.
PEDRO: Will that English girl that he has met come with him?
JUAN: He says that he has invted her, but he doesn´t know if she will accept although he thinks that she is interested. He met her the first day of the holidays.
PEDRO: How lucky to be on holiday! I can´t go until next month. And you?
JUAN: I will also have my holidays in August. I´ll go to London to see if I am as lucky as José.
PEDRO: It´s a good idea. I will probably come with you.
JUAN: Wait a minute! The other email is from my aunt Juana. She tells me she will give me five hundred euros for my birthday. I´ll pay. Lets go and celebrate. How do you fancy a couple of drinks?
PEDRO: Great!

PRACTICE D:

1. ¿Cuántos correos electrónicos hay para Juan? Hay dos.
2. ¿Cuándo salió José de vacaciones? Salió de vacaciones hace cinco días.
3. ¿Adónde fue? Fue a Londrés.
4. ¿Qué dice en el email? Dice que hace mucho frio pero se divierte mucho.
5. ¿A quién ha concido? Ha conocido a una chica inglesa muy simpática.
6. ¿Para dónde saldrán mañana? Saldrán para el Norte.
7. ¿Dónde trabajaba Pedro con José? Trabajaba con José en el banco.
8. ¿Cuándo volverá José? Llegará en Barcelona la semana que viene.
9. ¿Lo acompañará la chica inglesa que ha conocido? La ha invitado, pero no sabe si aceptará.
10. ¿Cuándo la conoció? La conoció el primer día de las vacaciones.
11. ¿Cuándo podrán Pedro y Juan ir de vacaciones? Podrán ir de vacaciones el mes que viene, en agosto.
12. ¿Adónde irá Juan? Irá a Londrés.
13. ¿Quién a lo mejor lo acompañará? Pedro a lo mejor lo acompañará.

14. ¿De quién es el otro email? El otro email es de su tia Juana.
15. ¿Cuánto dice que le dará para su cumpleaños? Dice que le dará quinientos euros.

8. FUTURE SIMPLE- THE NEW HOUSE

PRACTICE A:

VERB	INFINITIVE	SPANISH	TENSE	PERSON
1. I have bought	To buy	comprar	p. perfect	1st p.sing
2. is	To be	estar	present	3rd p.sing
3. is	To be	ser	present	3rd p.sing
4. is	To be	ser	present	3rd p.sing
5. Will you live	To live	vivir	future simp.	2nd p.sing
6. I will only spend	To spend	pasar	future simp.	1st p.sing
7. I will show	To show	mostrar	future simp.	1st p.sing
8. are not	To be	estar	present	3rd p.plural
9. they will install	To install	instalar	future simp.	3rd p.plural
10. is	To be	ser	present	3rd p.sing
11. will you furnish	To furnish	amueblar	future simp.	2nd p.sing
12. I will furnish	To furnish	amueblar	future simp.	1st p.sing
13. I haven´t got	To have got	tener	present	1st p.sing
14. to buy	To buy	comprar	infinitive	
15. Will you decorate	To decorate	decorar	future simp.	2nd p.sing
16. I will bring	To bring	traer	future simp.	1st p.sing
17. I will place	To place	poner/colocar	future simp.	1st p.sing
18. will it be	To be	ser	future simp.	3rd p.sing
19. I will put	To put	poner	future simp.	1st p.sing
20. will go	To go	ir	future simp.	3rd p.sing
21. will be	To be	ser	future simp.	3rd p.sing
22. I will place	To place	poner/colocar	future simp.	1st p.sing
23. will occupy	To occupy	ocupar	future simp.	3rd p.sing
24. will connect	To connect	conectar	future simp.	3rd p.sing
25. I don´t see	To see	ver	present	1st p.sing
26. Will you build	To build	construir	future simp.	2nd p.sing
27. It will be	To be	estar	future simp.	3rd p.sing
28. it will be	To be	ser	future simp.	3rd p.sing
29. to read	To read	leer	infinitive	
30. chat	To chat	charlar	infinitive	

31. I love	To love	encantar	present	3rd p.sing
32. Will you invite	To invite	invitar	future simp.	2nd p.sing
33. you have	To have	tener	present	2nd p.sing

PRACTICE B:

Alberto: He comprado una casa nueva en el campo. El pueblo está por allí y esa casa al lado del rio es mia..
Manuel: !Qué bonita es! ¿Vivirás aqui todo el año?
Alberto: No, por ahora solo pasaré los fines de semana aqui. Por aqui y te la mostraré aunque las reformas no están terminadas todavía. La semana que viene instalarán la luz / electricidad y la calefacción.
Manuel: Este pasillo es muy grande. ¿Cómo lo amueblarás?
Alberto: Lo amueblaré poco a poco. No tengo mucho dinero ahora para comprar muchos muebles a la vez.
Manuel: La decorarás tú mismo?
Alberto: Sí, traeré algunos cuadros y adornos del piso/ apartamento. En frente de la puerta pondré/ colocaré un aparador español, y sobre un espejo.
Manuel: Esta habitación/ sala/ cuarto, ¿será el salón?
Alberto: Sí, de momento pondré/ colocaré un sofa y varias sillas. La tele/ televidsión irá por allí, y en ese rincón un bar.
Manuel: ¿Y cuál será tu despacho?
Alberto: Aquella habitación, al final del pasillo. Delamte de mi mesa de trabajo pondré/ colocaré una estantería grande que ocupará toda la pared. El despacho conectará con mi dormitorio.
Manuel: No veo ninguna chimenea. ¿Construirás una?
Alberto: !Por supuesto! Estará en el salóñ. En invierno será genial leer y charlar delante del fuego.
Manuel: Me encanta tu casa. ¿Me invitarás alguna vez?
Alberto: Claro que sí. Aqui tienes tu casa también.

PRACTICE C:

1. ¿Dónde está la casa nueva de Alberto? Está al lado del rio.
2. ¿Vivirá allí todo el año? No, por ahora solo pasará los fines de semana aquí.
3. ¿Están terminadas las reformas todavía? Las reformas no están terminadas todavía.
4. ¿Qué le instalarán la semana que viene? La semana que viene le instalarán la luz / electricidad y la calefacción.

5. ¿Cómo amueblará el pasillo? Lo amueblará poco a poco.
6. ¿Llamará Alberto a un decorador o decorará la casa él mismo? Lo decorará él mismo.
7. ¿Qué pondrá/colocará en el salón? Pondrá/ colocará un sofa y varias sillas.
8. ¿Cuál será su despacho y con qué habitación conectará? Aquella habitación, al final del pasillo. Conectará con su dormitorio.
9. ¿Construirá una chimenea? ¿Dónde y por qué? Estará en el salón. En invierno será genial leer y charlar delante del fuego.
10. Describe tu casa. **FREE ANSWER**

9. FUTURE SIMPLE-TRANSLATION USING IRREGULAR VERBS.

PRACTICE A:

VERB	INFINITIVE	SPANISH	TENSE	PERSON
1. can you	To "can"	poder	present	2nd p. sing
2. pack	To pack	hacer	infinitive	
3. I have to	To have to	Tener que	present	
4. go	To go	ir	infinitive	
5. will you leave	To leave	salir	future	2nd p. sing
6. lunch	To have lunch	comer	infinitive	
7. I will go	To go	ir	future	
8. I will catch	To catch	coger	future	
9. Will you be	To be	estar	future	2nd p. sing
10. I hope	To hope	esperar	present	1st p. sing
11. to be	To be	estar	infinitive	
12. I will have to	To have to	tener que	future	2nd p. sing
13. discuss	To discuss	discutir	infinitive	
14. will only take	To to take	tardar	future	
15. I will come home	To come home	volver a casa	future	1st p. sing
16. I will tell	To tell	decir	future	1st p. sing
17. I will pack	To pack	hacer	future	1st p. sing
18. it is	To be	ser	present	3rd p. sing
19. travelling	To travel	viajar	infinitive	
20. you go	To go	ir	present	2nd p. sing
21. you know	To know	saber	present	2nd p. sing

22. I don´t like	To like	gustar	present	3rd p. sing
23. to go	To go	ir	infinitive	
24. It´s	To be	ser	present	3rd p. sing
25. You are	To be/have	tener miedo	present	2nd p. sing
26. you will go	To go	ir	future	2nd p. sing
27. It is	To be	ser	present	3rd p. sing
28. to travel	To travel	viajar	infinitive	
29. I will be able to	To be able	poder	future	1st p. sing
30. relax	To relax	descansar	infinitive	
31. I will bring	To bring	traer	future	1st p. sing
32. I´ll see	To see	ver	future	1st p. sing

PRACTICE B:

PEDRO: Hola Carmen. Por favor puedes hacerme una maleta. Tengo que ir de viaje a París.
CARMEN: ¿Cuándo saldrás?
PEDRO: Después de comer iré a Barcelona allí cogeré el tren a Paris.
CARMEN: ¿Estarás en Paris muchos días?
PEDRO: No, espero estar allí solo un par de días. Tendré que discutir una cosas importantes que solo me tardarán un rato/ tiempo corto. Volveré a casa el viernes y te diré todo.
CARMEN: Entonces haré la maleta pequeña para tí, es más cómodo para viajar. ¿Por qué no vas en avión?
PEDRO: !No! Sabes que no me gusta ir en avión. Es peligroso.
CARMEN: Tienes miedo de los aviones. Entonces irás en coche-cama?
PEDRO: Claro que sí. Es la manera más cómoda y segura para viajar. Podré descansar bastantes horas.
CARMEN: Vale/ bien. Traeré tu maleta a la oficina en bréve/ dentro de poco. Te veré entonces.
PEDRO: Vale/ Bien/ Bueno. Hasta entonces.

PRACTICE C:

1. ¿Tiene que ir Pedro de viaje? Sí, tiene que ir de viaje.
2. ¿Adónde viajará Pedro? A París.
3. ¿Cuándo saldrá? Después de comer.
4. ¿Pasará mucho tiempo en París? No, esperoa estar allí solo un par de días.
5. ¿Qué tendrá que discutir? Tendrá que discutir una cosas importantes.

6. ¿Cuándo volverá a casa y qué hará? Volverá a casa el viernes y le dirá todo.
7. ¿En qué viajará? En coche-cama.
8. ¿Qué hará Carmen para él y por qué? Hará la maleta pequeña para él, por qué es más cómodo para viajar.
9. ¿Por qué no viajará en avión? Tiene miedo de los aviones.
10. ¿Por qué prefiere el tren? Es la manera más cómoda y segura para viajar.
11. ¿De dónde irá a París? De Barcelona.
12. ¿Adónde llevará Carmen la maleta? Traerá/ llevará la maleta a la oficina.
13. ¿Dónde estará el próximo lugar a dónde viajarás? FREE ANSWER
14. ¿Llevarás much eqipaje contigo? FREE ANSWER

10. CONDITIONAL.

PRACTICE A:

1. Comería las galletas, pero estoy a régimen.
2. ¿Te casarías con él?
3. ¿Adónde iríais?
4. No vivirían en esa casa porque es demasiado pequeña.
5. ¿Entregarías los libros a nuestra casa?
6. Seríais mis estudiantes.
7. Lo perderían.
8. Cantaríamos una canción pero estamos resfriados.
9. Me levantaría pero estoy demasiada cómoda.
10. Saben que les darías el dinero mañana.
11. ¿Por qué comería alguien eso?
12. ¿Por qué no me acostaría a esa hora?
13. No tocarías el piano delante de toda esa gente.
14. No pagarían mucho por la casa.
15. No se acostaría antes de las once.
16. No me bañaría en el verano.

PRACTICE B:

1. haber- to have/auxiliary- habría, habrías, habría, habríamos, habríais, habrían.
2. poder- to be able- podría, podrías, podría, podríamos, podríais, podrían.
3. querer- to want-querría, querrías, querría, querríamos, querríais, querrían.
4. saber- to know- sabría, sabrías, sabría, sabríamos, sabríais, sabrían.
5. poner- to put- pondría, pondrías, pondría, podríamos, pondríais, pondrían.

6. salir- to leave/go out- saldría, saldrías, saldría, saldríamos, saldríais, saldrían.
7. tener- to have- tendría, tendrías, tendría, tendríamos, tendríais, tendrían.
8. valer- to be worth- valdría, valdrías, valdría, valdríamos, valdríais, valdrían
9. venir- to come- vendría, vendrías, vendría, vendríamos, vendríais, vendrían.
10. decir- to say/tell- diría, dirías, diría, diríamos, diríais, dirían.
11. hacer- to do/ make- haría, harías, haría, haríamos, haríais, harían.

PRACTICE C: Free answers.

PRACTICE E:

VERB	INFINITIVE	SPANISH	TENSE	PERSON
1. was	To be	ser	imperfect	1st p.sing
2. I loved	To love	encantar	imperfect	3rd p. sing
3. to read	To leer	leer	infinitive	
4. I had	To have	tener	imperfect	1st p.sing
5. was	To be	ser	imperfect	3rd p. sing
6. could	To be able	poder	imperfect	3rd p. sing
7. grant	To grant	conceder	infinitive	
8. would I ask for?	To ask for	pedir	conditional	1st p.sing
9. I would ask	To ask for	pedir	conditional	1st p.sing
10. I know	To know	To know	present	1st p.sing
11. he wouldn´t do	To do	hacer	conditional	3rd p. sing
12. would be	To be	ser	conditional	3rd p. sing
13. would be able	To be able	poder	conditional	3rd p. sing
14. to speak	To speak	hablar	infinitive	
15. would have	To have	tener	conditional	1st p.plural
16. I would marry	To marry	casarse	conditional	1st p.sing
17. would be	To be	ser	conditional	3rd p. sing
18. would have to	To have to	tener que	conditional	3rd p. sing
19. to suffer	To suffer	sufrir	infinitive	
20. There would be no	There is/are	haber	conditional	3rd p. sing
21. There would be no	There is/are	haber	conditional	3rd p. sing
22. There would be no	There is/are	haber	conditional	3rd p. sing
23. would be	To be	ser	conditional	3rd p. sing

PRACTICE E:

Cuando era joven, me encantaba leer y tenía una imaginación viva. Una de mis personajes favoritas era el Genio de la Lámpara porque podía conceder tres deseos a la gente. ¿Qué pediría yo? Primero, le pediría cien más desos, pero sé que no haría esto. Entonces, estos serían mis tres deseos. 1. Mi perro podría hablar y ella y yo tendríamos conversaciones largas. 2. Me casaría con el hombre de mis sueños. 3. Y el deseo más importante sería facíl… nadie en el mundo tendría que sufrir más. No habría pobreza, no habría tristeza. El mundo sería perfecto…

11. FUTURE/CONDITIONAL CONVERSATION PRACTICE

PRACTICE A:

1. ¿Qué harás este Navidad?
2. ¿Adónde irás el fin de semana que viene?
3. ¿Con quién habalarás mañana?
4. ¿Qué comprarías con diez mil euros?
5 ¿Cómo practicarás español después de este curso?
6. ¿Cambiarías algo en tu vida?
7. ¿Cuánto tiempo esperarías en una cola?
8. ¿Estarás en España dentro de dos años?
9. ¿Qué, si algo, cambiarías de tu mismo/a?
10. ¿Sería mejor para la economía española salir del euro?
11. ¿Qué tiempo hará en verano?
12. Adónde irás de vacaciones el año que viene?
13. ¿Adónde te gustaría visitar en España?
14. ¿Con cuál persona famosa te gustaría más pasar el día?
15. ¿Cuál trabajo no harías?
16. ¿Qué cocinarás el domingo?
17. ¿Qué sería tu regalo perfecto?
18. ¿Hablarás español esta noche?
19. ¿Cuándo necesitarías un interprete
20. ¿Qué eligirías en un restaurante indio?

FREE ANSWERS

12. SER/ESTAR- FUTURE/CONDITIONAL.

PRACTICE A:

1. Estaría allí a las 5.
2. Serían muy altos en cinco años.
3. Estaria feliz, pero no tengo dinero.
4. Sería enfermera pero no le gusta la sangre.
5. Estarían muy enfadados.
6. Estarías allí pero no hay más plazos.
7. Estaríamos en el hotel el sábado.
8. Barcelona sería una ciudad muy bonita para visitar.
9. ¿Estarías en casa esta noche?
10. ¿Cuánto sería para dos adultos y dos niños?

PRACTICE B:

1. ¿Estarías en Sevilla para Semana Santa?
2. Creo que será buen partido mañana.
3. Seremos los primeros en la cola.
4. Sería buen precio, pero no funciona.
5. No estaría aqui, pero lo llamé ayer para invitarlo.
6. Será muy simpático.
7. ¿Estarías contentos con el coche?
8. Serían ricos, pero perdieron todo su dinero en el casino.
9. Eso sería estupendo.
10. Sería la primera Presidenta de los Estados Unidos.

13. DEMONSTRATIVE ADJECTIVES AND PRONOUNS.

PRACTICE A:

1. Este libro es mio, pero ése es suyo.
2. Aquella casa es bonita, pero ésta es más bonita.
3. Estos zapatos eran mios y ésos eran suyos.
4. Aquello chico era mi vecino, y éste es su amigo.
5. Esa mujer es mi compañera, pero aquéllas trabajaban en la oficina al lado.
6. Estos libros son en español pero ésos son en inglés.
7. Aquel teléfono no funcionó ayer pero este sí.
8. Aquel perro estaba en el parque anoche pero ése no.
9. Ese coche siempre ha funcionado bien pero éste nunca ha arrancado.
10. Aquel hombre es francés pero este es alemán.

PRACTICE B:

1. Esto es estupendo.
2. ¿Qué es eso?
3. Nunca hago eso.
4. ¿Hiciste esto?
5. Eso fue terrible.
6. Esto es por que no fumo.
7. Eso es por que las relaciones son tan difíciles.
8. ¿Quién dijo eso?
9. ¿Cuándo dije eso?
10. ¿Quién quería eso?

14. INDIRECT OBJECT PRONOUNS.

PRACTICE A:

1. Me lo dijo ayer.
2. No nos los comprabamos a menudo.
3. No nos lo mandaron.
4. No se lo hacemos cada día.
5. Te lo pagó en efectivo.
6. Me lo va a enviar mañana / Va a enviarmelo mañana.
7. Se lo canté.
8. Se lo tuvimos que vender/ Tuvimos que venderselo.
9. Me lo puedes mandar por email/ Puedes mandarmelo por email.
10. Te lo debes comprar/ Debes comprartelo.
11. No nos lo necesitó pagar anteayer.
12. ¿Por qué me la das?
13. Se lo está preparando/ Está preparandoselo.
14. Se los compraba.
15. Te los estoy guardando/ Estoy guardandotelos.

PRACTICE B:

VERB	INFINITIVE	SPANISH	TENSE	PERSON
1, I had	To have	tener	preterite	1st p.sing.
2. he lived	To live	vivir	imperfecto	3rd p. sing.
3. he seemed	To seem	parecer	imperfecto	3rd p. sing.
4. to be	To be	ser	infinitive	
5. I wanted	To want	querer	imperfecto	1st p.sing.
6. to give	To give	dar	infinitive	

7. I made	To make	hacer	preterite	1st p.sing.
8. wrote	To write	escribir	preterite	1st p.sing.
9. said	To say	decir	preterite	3rd p. sing.
10. I took	To take	llevar	preterite	1st p.sing.
11. left	To leave	dejar	preterite	1st p.sing.
12. called	To call	llamar	preterite	3rd p. sing.
13. thanked	To thank	dar las gracias	preterite	3rd p. sing.
14. he gave	To give	dar	preterite	3rd p. sing.
15. I put	To put	poner	preterite	1st p.sing.
16. they were	To be	ser	imperfecto	3rd p.plural
17. see	To see	ver	present	1st p.sing.
18. I make	To make	hacer	present	1st p.sing.
19. we eat	To eat	comer	present	1st p.plural
20. he buys	To buy	comprar	present	3rd p. sing.
21. he brings	To bring	traer	present	3rd p. sing.
22. I put	To put	poner	present	1st p.sing.
23. take	To take	llevar	present	1st p.sing.
24. he says	To say	decir	present	3rd p. sing.
25. he gives	To give	dar	present	3rd p. sing.
26. I made	To make	hacer	preterite	1st p.sing.
27. I improved	To improve	mejorar	preterite	1st p.sing.
28. I want	To want	querer	present	1st p.sing.
29. to improve	To improve	mejorar	infinitive	
30. it was	To be	ser	preterite	3rd p. sing.
31. he came	To come	venir	preterite	3rd p. sing.
32. to live	To live	vivir	infinitive	
33. he gave	To give	dar	preterite	3rd p. sing.
34. he bought	To buy	comprar	preterite	3rd p. sing.
35. I will wear	To wear	llevar	future	1st p.sing.
36. we will get married	To get married	casarse	future	1st p.plural

PRACTICE C:

Una vez tuve un vecino nuevo. Vivía al lado de mí. Siempre me parecía ser muy simpático. Quería darle algo bonito. Le hice una tarta/ hice una tarta para él y le escribí una nota que dijo "bienvenido a la calle". La llevé a su casa y la dejé fuera de su puerta. El día siguiente me llamó por teléfono y me dio las gracias por la tarta. Me dio unas flores, y las puse en un florero en la mesa en el salón. Eran muy bonitas.

Ahora lo veo cada día y los fines de semana le hago una tarta y la comemos juntos. Cada domingo me compra flores y me las trae, las pongo en un florero y lo llevo al salón. Dice que me las da porque cuando le hice aquella tarta, mejoré su vida. (Se la) Quiero mejorar(sela) para siempre. Fue buen día para nosotros cuando vino a vivir en mi calle. Me dio un anillo ayer y me lo compró en una tienda muy cara. Lo llevaré para siempre y en el verano nos casaremos.

15. POSESSIVE ADJECTIVES AND PRONOUNS

PRACTICE A:

1, Es mi teléfono. Es mio.
2. Era/fue tu comida. Era/ fue tuya.
3. Era/ fue su marido, fue/era suyo.
4. Han sido nuestros vecinos. Han sido nuestros.
5. Son sus mesas. Son suyas.
6. Eran vuestros perros. Eran vuestros
7. Han sido mis amigos. Han sido mios.
8. Era su abogado. Era suyo.
9. Eramos sus medicos. Eramos suyos.
10. Han sido tus problemas. Han sido tuyos.
11. Un amigo/a mio/a trabaja aqui.
12. Algunos amigos suyos vivían allí.
13. Un compañero nuestro tenía una casa en España.
14. Nunca han hablado más con él porque es un enimigo suyo.
15. Ese restaurant siempre ha sido un favorito mio.

PRACTICE B:

Estaba muy molestada porque Sarah tenía mi bolso. Dijo que era suyo. Pero sé que era mio porque tiene mis iniciales. Sarah roba todo. Nada en su casa es suya. Muchas cosas son mias. Por ejemplo todos sus zapatos son mios, el anillo de plata en su dedo es mio,. Tres de sus bufandas y guantes son mios, hasta algo se la comida en el armario es mia. ¿Qué puedo hacer? La ley dice que posesión es noventa y nueve porciento de la ley. Entonces, todo es mio.

16. VERB TABLES- REVISION OF TENSES.

PRACTICE A:

1. HABLAR - to speak

PRESENT	P.PERFECT	PRETRITE	IMPERFECT	FUTURE	FUT.COND.
hablo	he hablado	hablé	hablaba	hablaré	hablaría
hablas	has	hablaste	hablabas	hablarás	hablarías
habla	ha	habló	hablaba	hablará	hablaría
hablamos	hemos	hablamos	hablábamos	hablaremos	hablaríamos
habláis	habéis	hablasteis	hablabais	hablaréis	hablaríais
hablan	han	hablaron	hablaban	hablarán	hablarían

2. PONER - to put

PRESENT	P.PERFECT	PRETRITE	IMPERFECT	FUTURE	FUT.COND.
pongo	he puesto	puse	ponía	pondré	pondría
pones	has	pusiste	ponías	pondrás	pondrías
pone	ha	puso	ponía	pondrá	pondría
ponemos	hemos	pusimos	poníamos	pondremos	pondríamos
ponéis	habéis	pusisteis	poníais	pondréis	pondríais
ponen	han	pusieron	Ponían	pondrán	pondrían

3. ESTAR - to be

PRESENT	P.PERFECT	PRETERITE	IMPERFECT	FUTURE	FUT.COND.
estoy	he estado	estuve	estaba	estaré	estaría
estás	has	estuviste	estabas	estarás	estarías
está	ha	estuvo	estaba	estará	estaría
estámos	hemos	estuvimos	éstabamos	estaremos	estaríamos
estáis	habéis	estuvisteis	estabais	estaréis	estaríais
están	han	estuvieron	estaban	estarán	estarían

4. SER - to be

PRESENT	P.PERFECT	PRETERITE	IMPERFECT	FUTURE	FUT.COND.
soy	he sido	fui	era	seré	sería
eres	has	fuiste	eras	serás	serías
es	ha	fue	era	será	sería
somos	hemos	fuimos	éramos	seremos	seríamos
sois	habéis	fuisteis	erais	seréis	seríais
son	han	fueron	eran	serán	serían

5. LEER - to read

PRESENT	P.PERFECT	PRETERITE	IMPERFECT	FUTURE	FUT.COND.
leo	he leido	leí	leía	leeré	leería
lees	has	leiste	leías	leerás	leerías
lee	ha	leyó	leía	leerá	leería
leemos	hemos	leimos	leíamos	leeremos	leeríamos
leéis	habéis	leisteis	leíais	leeréis	leeríais
leen	han	leyeron	leían	leerán	leerían

6. SUBIR - to go up

PRESENT	P.PERFECT	PRETERITE	IMPERFECT	FUTURE	FUT.COND.
subo	he subido	subí	subía	subiré	subiría
subes	has	subiste	subías	subirás	subirías
sube	ha	subió	subía	subirá	subiría
subimos	hemos	subimos	subíamos	subiremos	subiríamos
subís	habéis	subisteis	subíais	subiréis	subiríais
suben	han	subieron	subían	subirán	subirían

7. VOLVER - to return

PRESENT	P.PERFECT	PRETERITE	IMPERFECT	FUTURE	FUT.COND.
vuelvo	he vuelto	volví	volvía	volveré	volvería
vuelves	has	volviste	volvías	volverás	volverías
vuelve	ha	volvió	volvía	volverá	volvería
volvemos	hemos	volvimos	volvíamos	volveremos	volveríamos
volvéis	habéis	volvisteis	volvíais	volveréis	volveríais
vuelven	han	volvieron	volvían	volverán	volverían

8. IR - to go

PRESENT	P.PERFECT	PRETERITE	IMPERFECT	FUTURE	FUT.COND.
voy	he ido	fui	iba	iré	iría
vas	has	fuiste	ibas	irás	irías
va	ha	fue	iba	irá	iría
vamos	hemos	fuimos	íbamos	iremos	iríamos
vais	habéis	fusteis	ibais	iréis	iríais
van	han	fueron	iban	irán	irían

9. CANTAR - to sing

PRESENT	P.PERFECT	PRETERITE	IMPERFECT	FUTURE	FUT.COND.
canto	he cantado	canté	cantaba	cantaré	cantaría
cantas	has	cantaste	cantabas	cantarás	cantarías
canta	ha	cantó	cantaba	cantará	cantaría
cantamos	hemos	cantamos	cantábamos	cantaremos	cantaríamos
cantáis	habéis	cantasteis	cantabais	cantaréis	cantaríais
cantan	han	cantaron	cantaban	cantarán	cantarían

10. QUERER - to want

PRESENT	P.PERFECT	PRETERITE	IMPERFECT	FUTURE	FUT.COND.
quiero	he querido	quise	quería	querré	querría
quieres	has	quisiste	querías	querrás	querrías
quiere	ha	quiso	quería	querrá	querría
queremos	hemos	quisimos	queríamos	querremos	querríamos
queréis	habéis	quisisteis	queríais	querréis	querrías
quieren	han	quisieron	querían	querrán	querrían

11. PODER - to be able

PRESENT	P.PERFECT	PRETERITE	IMPERFECT	FUTURE	FUT.COND.
puedo	he podido	pude	podía	podré	podría
puedes	has	pudiste	podías	podrás	podrías
puede	ha	pudo	podía	podrá	podría
podemos	hemos	pudimos	podíamos	podremos	podríamos
podéis	habéis	pudisteis	podíais	podréis	podríais
pueden	han	pudieron	podían	podrán	podrían

8. DESPERTARSE - to wake up

PRESENT	P.PRFECT	PRETERITE	IMPERFECT	FUTURE	FUT.COND
me despierto	me he despertado	me desperté	me despertaba	me despertaré	me despertaría
te despiertas	te has	te despertaste	te despertabas	te despertarás	te despertarías
se despierta	se ha	se despertó	se despertaba	se despertará	se despertaría
nos despertamos	nos hemos	nos despertamos	nos despertábamos	nos despertaremos	nos despertaríamos
os despertáis	os habéis	os despertasteis	os despertabais	os despertaréis	os despertaríais
se despiertan	se han	se despertaron	se despertaban	se despertarán	se despertarían

9. ESCRIBIR - to write

PRESENT	P.PERFECT	PRETERITE	IMPERFECT	FUTURE	FUT.COND.
escribo	he escrito	escribí	escribía	escribiré	escribiría
escribes	has	escribiste	escribías	escribirás	escribirías
escribe	ha	escribió	escribía	escribirá	escribiría
escribimos	hemos	escribimos	escribíamos	escribiremos	escribiríamos
escribís	habéis	escribisteis	escribíais	escribiréis	escribiríais
escriben	han	escribieron	escribían	escribirán	escribirían

10. ACOSTARSE - to go to bed

PRESENT	P.PERFECT	PRETERITE	IMPERFECT	FUTURE	FUT.COND.
me acuesto	me he acostado	me acosté	me acostaba	me acostaré	me acostaría
te acuestas	te has	te acostaste	te acostabas	te acostarás	te acostarías
se acuesta	se ha	se acostó	se acostaba	se acostará	se acostaría
nos acostamos	nos hemos	nos acostamos	nos acostábamos	nos acostaremos	nos acostaríamos
os acostáis	os habéis	os acostasteis	os acostabais	os acostaréis	os acostaríais
se acuestan	se han	se acostaron	se acostaban	se acostarán	se acostarían

11. VENIR - to come

PRESENT	P.PERFECT	PRETERITE	IMPERFECT	FUTURE	FUT.COND.
vengo	he venido	vine	venía	vendré	vendría
vienes	has	viniste	venías	vendrás	vendrías
viene	ha	vino	venía	vendrá	vendría
venimos	hemos	vinimos	veníamos	vendremos	vendríamos
venís	habéis	vinisteis	veníais	vendréis	vendríais
vienen	han	vinieron	venían	vendrán	vendrían

12. DECIR - to say/tell

PRESENT	P.PERFECT	PRETRITE	IMPERFECT	FUTURE	FUT.COND.
digo	he dicho	dije	decía	diré	diría
dices	has	dijiste	decías	dirás	dirías
dice	ha	dijo	decía	dirá	diría
decimos	hemos	dijimos	decíamos	diremos	diríamos
decís	habéis	dijisteis	decíais	diréis	diríais
dicen	han	dijeron	decían	dirán	dirían

13. PENSAR - to think

PRESENT	P.PERFECT	PRETERITE	IMPERFECT	FUTURE	FUT.COND.
pienso	he pensado	pensé	pensaba	pensaré	pensaría
piensas	has	pensaste	pensabas	pensarás	pensarías
piensa	ha	pensó	pensaba	pensará	pensaría
pensamos	hemos	pensamos	pensábamos	pensaremos	pensaríamos
pensáis	habéis	pensasteis	pensabais	pensaréis	pensaríais
piensan	han	pensaron	pensaban	pensarán	pensarían

14. TENER - to have

PRESENT	P.PERFECT	PRETERITE	IMPERFECT	FUTURE	FUT.COND.
tengo	he tenido	tuve	tenía	tendré	tendría
tienes	has	tuviste	tenías	tendrás	tendrías
tiene	ha	tuvo	tenía	tendrá	tendría
tenemos	hemos	tuvimos	teníamos	tendremos	tendríamos
tenéis	habéis	tuvisteis	teníais	tendréis	tendríais
tienen	han	tuvieron	tenían	tendrán	tendrían

15. MIRAR - to look at

PRESENT	P.PERFECT	PRETERITE	IMPERFECT	FUTURE	FUT.COND.
miro	he mirado	miré	miraba	miraré	miraría
miras	has	miraste	mirabas	mirarás	mirarías
mira	ha	miró	miraba	mirará	miraría
miramos	hemos	miramos	mirábamos	miraremos	miraríamos
miráis	habéis	mirasteis	mirabais	miraréis	miraríais
miran	han	miraron	miraban	mirarán	mirarían

16. COGER - to get/catch

PRESENT	P.PERFECT	PRETERITE	IMPERFECT	FUTURE	FUT.COND.
cojo	he cogido	cogí	cogía	cogeré	cogería
coges	has	cogiste	cogías	cogerás	cogerías
coge	ha	cogió	cogía	cogerá	cogería
cogemos	hemos	cogimos	cogíamos	cogeremos	cogeríamos
cogéis	habéis	cogisteis	cogíais	cogeréis	cogeríais
cogen	han	cogieron	cogían	cogerán	cogerían

17. CEPILLARSE - to brush

PRESENT	P.PERFECT	PRETERITE	IMPERFECT	FUTURE	FUT.COND.
me cepillo	me he cepillado	me cepillé	me cepillaba	me cepillaré	me cepillaría
te cepillas	te has	te cepillaste	te cepillabas	te cepillarás	te cepillarías
se cepilla	se ha	se cepilló	se cepillaba	se cepillará	se cepillaría
nos cepillamos	nos hemos	nos cepillamos	nos cepillábamos	nos cepillaremos	nos cepillaríamos
os cepilláis	os habéis	os cepillasteis	os cepillabais	os cepillaréis	os cepillaríais
se cepillan	se han	se cepillaron	se cepillaban	se cepillarán	se cepillarían

18. ANDAR - to walk

PRESENT	P.PERFECT	PRETERITE	IMPERFECT	FUTURE	FUT.COND.
ando	he andado	anduve	andaba	andaré	andaría
andas	has	anduviste	andabas	andarás	andarías
anda	ha	anduvo	andaba	andará	andaría
andamos	hemos	anduvimos	andabámos	andaremos	andaríamos
andáis	habéis	anduvisteis	andabais	andaréis	andaríais
andan	han	anduvieron	andaban	andarán	andarían

19. COMPARTIR - to share

PRESENT	P.PERFECT	PRETERITE	IMPERFECT	FUTURE	FUT.COND
comparto	he compartido	compartí	compartía	compartiré	compartiría
compartes	has	compartiste	compartías	compartirás	compartirías
comparte	ha	compartió	compartía	compartirá	compartiría
compartimos	hemos	compartimos	compartíamos	compartiremos	compartiríamos
compartís	habéis	compartisteis	compartíais	compartiréis	compartiríais
comparten	han	compartieron	compartían	compartirán	compartirían

20. JUGAR- to play					
PRESENT	P.PERFECT	PRETERITE	IMPERFECT	FUTURE	FUT.COND.
juego	he jugado	jugué	jugaba	jugaré	jugaría
juegas	has	jugaste	jugabas	jugarás	jugarías
juega	ha	jugó	jugaba	jugará	jugaría
jugamos	hemos	jugamos	jugábamos	jugaremos	jugaríamos
jugáis	habéis	jugasteis	jugabais	jugaréis	jugaríais
juegan	han	jugaron	jugaban	jugarán	jugarían

17. "PARA" OR "POR"? PART 1- "PARA"

PRACTICE A:

1. You(s) have to pay the bill by the 31st of August. (e)
2. Carlos had a ring for her. (b)
3. I put the TV on to watch the news. (d)
4. This summer we are going to England. (c)
5. For him, María was the prettiest girl in the class. (g)
6. One has to/ it is necessary to work hard to get good marks. (d)
7. Ana went to singing classes. (d)
8. This cream would be for your face and that one would be for your hands. (a)
9. This café is cheap for a bar on the beach. (f)
10. This paper is for wrapping presents. (d)
11. To us, it's great to go to the cinema on Saturdays. (g)
12. They were studying to be teachers. (d)
13. There was a lot of rain for spring. (f)
14. For me, the heat is better than the cold. (g)
15. You should buy flowers for your girlfriend on the 14th of February. (b)
16. This is for washing clothes. (d)
17. I have work for next year. (e)
18. We leave for the office at 9 o´ clock. (c)
19. This chair will be for the patio. (a)
20. José is very intelligent for a boy of 11 years old. (f)

PRACTICE B:

1. Esta casa es perfecta para nosotros. (g)
2. Necesitabamos una mesa nueva para el comedor. (a)
3. No es importante tener coche para alguna gente. (g)
4. Estos zapatos serán para andar en el campo. (d)

5. Tienen que leer el libro para jueves. (e)
6. Fue al bar para olvidar sus problemas. (d)
7. Salieron para los Estados Unidos ayer. (c)
8. ¿Estudias para ser contable? (d)
9. Era muy educado para un adolescente. (f)
10. ¿Podrás escribir la carta para el martes? (e)
11. Esta carne es para los perros. (a)
12. Para mí, prefiero el coche rojo pero para él, prefiere el negro. (g)
13. Trabajaba los domingos para ganar más dinero. (d)
14. ¿A qué hora sales para el trabajo? (c)

18. "PARA" OR "POR"? PART 2- "POR".

PRACTICE A:

1. She used to run for half an hour every day.
2. We went to Amsterdam by plane.
3. We walked through the Shopping Centre but we didn´t buy anything.
4. We paid two hundred euros for the sofa.
5. The car goes at sixty miles an hour.
6. I looked for the cat everywhere withpout finding it.
7. I don´t have any feelings for you.
8. She always worked in the evening.
9. Thanks for your help.
10. He/she always gets good marks for studying hard.
11. I have a cough, can you speak for me?
12. I stopped by the supermarket before going to the cinema.
13. We go to the theatre on Saturday night.
14. I won´t want to pay more than fifteen euros for a menu of the day.
15. They always buy food separately.
16. We used to drive around the country on Sundays.
17. You can send me the information by fax.
18. No one works for me when I am ill.
19. Elton John is famous for his songs.
20. Now he/she is broke because of buying so many things.

PRACTICE B:

1. Fuimos al colegio/instituto por autobús.
2. Puedes tener esos zapatos por veinte euros.
3. Tenía por lo menos veinte gatos.

4. Siempre pasearé por el parque por la mañana.
5. Leíamos los periódicos por una hora cada mañana.
6. ¿Puedes trabajar por María hoy? Está enferma.
7. Voy al supermercado por leche, pan y huevos.
8. Miraba el futból cada miércoles por la noche.
9. No puede tocar el gato por sus alergias.
10. Gracias por nada.
11. Merecía una medalla por dar tanto a los demás.
12. Noventa porciento de los dentistas recomendarán esta pasta de dientes.
13. Pasa por mi casa de vez en cuando.
14. Tengo mucho cariño por él.

19. "PARA" OR "POR"? -COMPARISON A.

PRACTICE A:

1. Tuve un par de cosas para él.
2. Juan es muy simpático para un hombre tan guapo.
3. Muchas gracias por los chocolates.
4. Me gusta pasear por todas las tiendas en un pueblo.
5. El concierto empezará a las 9, queremos llegar a las ocho y media.
6. No me gustan estos zapatos. Son para adolescentes.
7. Siempre tomo té por la mañana, pero tomo café por la tarde. Por la noche, tomo vino.
8. Esos cuadros eran para el dormitorio principal.
9. Siempre voy a Inglaterra por avión, nunca voy por coche.
10. Es una tienda muy cara. Cien euros por un par de zapatos!!
11. ¿Estás listo? Vamos para la fiesta ahora.
12. ¿Tienes hambre? Hay un restaurante por aqui.
13. No había colegio ayer por la nieve.
14. Carlos está enfermo hoy. ¿Puedes trabajar por él?
15. Debemos hacer ejercicio por lo menos tres veces por semana.
16. María prefería el verano, pero, para mí, el invierno es mejor.
17. No siento nada por él.
18. Contactaré con todos mis amigos por correo electrónico.
19. John Carpenter es famoso por sus películas.
20. Hablaba con mi novio por teléfono cada día.

20. "PARA" OR "POR"?- COMPARISON B.

PRACTICE A:

Ayer mi hermano vino a mi casa. Me dijo:
"Tengo una historia interesante para tí. Tenía un amigo que vivía en Alicante. Trabajaba para una empresa muy pequeña y por muy poco dinero. Siempre necesitaba más dinero para comida y facturas. Entonces cada viernes cuando compraba cigarillos pagaba cuatro euros más por dos
billetes de la lotería. Eligía los números por cumpleaños de sus amigos y familia. Hacía esto cada semana por más de quince años y nunca ganaba nada.

Durante este periódo, se casó. Sus padres les dieron el dinero para la boda y siempre les quería dar las gracias en absoluto por eso. Un año después, tuvieron su primer hijo y el segundo dos años después. Nunca tenían bastante dinero para todo que necesitaban y habían muchas cosas que sus hijos no podían tener.

La semana pasada, por primera vez, ganó. Ganó más de un millón de euros. Ahora tiene bastante dinero para comprar todo para él, sus amigos, y su familia. Están todos muy agredecidos por estas cosas. Normalmente, no pagaría más de dos mil euros por un coche, pero ahora, por ganar la lotería, mañana va a comprar un coche nuevo por cincuenta mil euros. Hermana, estoy muy contento por él.

21. "PARA" OR "POR"?- COMPARISON C.

PRACTICE A:

1. Para un viejo, tiene ideas muy jovenes.
2. Voy a mandar esta carta por avión.
3. No podía venir. Tuve que hacer la presentación por él.
4. Por fin, después de una espera larga, salimos del aeropuerto.
5. Necesito comprar un coche. Te daré mil euros por el tuyo.
6. España está conocida por su historia muy interesante.
7. Tuve que tomar medicina cuatro veces al día.
8. Mi padre trabaja para una empresa grande en alemania.
9. No tengo vasos para champán.
10. Aprendimos español para hablar con más gente.
11. Normalmente no hago mucho los sábados por la mañana.
12. Ayer el tiempo hizo fatal. Por eso, decidimos quedarnos en casa.
13. Me llamaron para invitarme a su boda.
14. Ella y Pepe están muy felices porque por fin se van a casar.
15. Y por eso, van a invitar a todos a su boda.

16. Tendrán una fiesta grande para celebrar.
17. Después de la boda, los dos saldrán para España.
18. Luisa se nació en los Estado Unidos pero para una Americana habla español bastante bien.
19. Mañana les agradeceré por invitarnos a la fiesta.
20. La semana pasada dieron una fiesta para celebrar su compromiso.
21. Amy, John, y yo decidimos darles cada uno cincuenta euros para poder comprarse un regalo bonito.
22. El sábado iremos al Centro Comercial para elegir algo.

22. TRANSLATION ENGLISH TO SPANISH MIXED TENSES.

PRACTICE A:

VERB	INFINITIVE	SPANISH	TENSE	PERSON
1. used to stay	To stay	quedarse	imperfect	3rd p.sing.
2. They would go	To go	ir	imperfect	3rd p.plur.
3. to fish	To fish	pescar	infinitive	

VERB	INFINITIVE	SPANISH	TENSE	PERSON
4. they would catch	To catch	coger	imperfect	3rd p.plur.
5. they will never forget	To forget	olvidar	future	3rd p.plur.
6. happened	To happen	pasar	preterite	3rd p.sing.
7. they didn't catch	To catch	coger	preterite	3rd p.plur.
8. It was	To be	Hacer (weather)	preterite	3rd p.sing.
9. they decided	To decide	decidir	preterite	3rd p.plur.
10. to spend	To spend	pasar	infinitive	
11. They took	To take	llevar	preterite	3rd p.plur.
12. They also took	To take	llevar	preterite	3rd p.plur.
13. they arrived	To arrive	llegar	preterite	3rd p.plur.
14. they put	To put	poner	preterite	3rd p.plur.
15. started	To start	empezar	preterite	3rd p.plur.
16. to fish	To fish	pescar	infinitive	
17. They could	To be able	poder	preterite	3rd p.plur.
18. see	To see	ver	infinitive	
19. an hour went by	To go by	pasar	preterite	3rd p.sing.
20. happened	To happen	ocurrir	preterite	3rd p.sing.
21. got up	To get up	levantarse	preterite	3rd p.plur.
22. shouting	To shout	gritar	gerund	
23. I have	To have	tener	present	1st p.sing.
24. I have	To have	tener	present	1st p.sing.

25. Carlos went	To go	ir	preterite	3rd p.sing.
26. to help	To help	ayudar	infinitive	
27. tripped	To trip	tropezar con	preterite	3rd p.plur.
28. were sitting	To sit	sentarse	imperfect	3rd p.plur.
29. fell	To fall	caerse	preterite	3rd p.sing.
30. he was	To be	ser	imperfect	3rd p.sing.
31. he managed	To manage	lograr	preterite	3rd p.sing.
32. to get out	To get out	salir	infinitive	
33. You´ll have to	To have to	tener que	future	2nd p.sing.
34. dry	To dry	secarse	infinitive	
35. said	To say	decir	preterite	3rd p.sing.
36. you will catch cold	To catch cold	resfriarse	future	2nd p.sing.
37. went	To go	ir	preterite	3rd p.plur.
38. catching	To catch	coger	infinitive	
39. changed	To change	cambiarse	preterite	3rd p.sing.
40. they ate	To eat	comer	preterite	3rd p.plur.
41. drank	To drink	beber	preterite	3rd p.plur.

PRACTICE B:

Pedro se quedaba con su amigo Carlos en las vacaciones de verano en el campo. A menudo iban a un lago cercano para pescar. Por lo general, cogían cuatro o cinco peces pero nunca olvidarán que les pasó ayer cuando no cogieron nada.

Hizo muy bueno, entonces decidieron pasar todo el día allí. Llevaron sus cañas de pescar, dos sillas, un paraguas y una nervera portátil con unas cervezas, agua y bocadillos. También llevaron los dos perros de Carlos, Pepe y Pepa con ellos. Cuando llegaron al lago pusieron sus cosas en la tierra al lado del lago y empezaron a pescar. Pudieron ver muchos peces grandes en el lago pero pasó una hora y no ocurrió nada.

De repente se levantó Pedro gritando- "Tengo algo, tengo algo!!". Carlos fue a ayudarlo, tropezó con uno de los perros que se sentaban a sus pies y se cayó en el agua. Con suerte, era nadador bueno y logró salir del agua sin mucha dificultad.

"Tendrás que secarse la ropa", dijo Pedro. "Si no, te resfriarás." Los dos hombres fueron a casa sin coger nada. Carlos se cambió la ropa y comieron los bocadillos y bebieron la cerveza en el patio de Carlos.

PRACTICE C:

1. ¿Con quién se quedaba Pedro en las vacaciones de verano? Se quedaba con su amigo Carlos.
2. ¿Adónde iban a menudo para pescar? Iban a un lago cercano.
3. ¿Cuántos peces cogieron normalmente? Normalmente cogieron cuatro o cinco peces.
4. ¿Qué nunca se olvidarán? Nunca se olvidarán que pasó ayer cuando no cogieron nada.
5. ¿Qué llevaron con ellos aparte de de sus cañas de pescar y por qué? Como hizo muy bueno, decidieron pasar todo el día allí. Llevaron dos sillas, un paraguas y una nervera portátil con unas cervezas, agua y bocadillos.
6. ¿Quiénes fueron con ellos también? Los dos perros de Carlos, Pepe y Pepa fueron con ellos también.
7. ¿Qué hicieron cuando llegaron al lago? Cuando llegaron al lago pusieron sus cosas el la tierra al lado del lago y empezaron a pescar.
8. ¿Qué pudieron ver en el lago? Pudieron ver muchos peces grandes en el lago.
9. ¿Qué hizo Pedro de repente? De repente Pedro se levantó.
10. ¿Qué gritaba? Gritaba "Tengo algo, tengo algo!!"
11. ¿Qué pasó cuando Carlos fue a ayudarlo? Tropezó con uno de los perros que se sentaban a sus pies y se cayó en el agua.
12. ¿Tuvo problemas en salir del agua? Con suerte, era nadador bueno y logró salir del agua sin mucha dificultad.
13. ¿Por qué dijo Pedro que tendrá que secarse la ropa? Si no, se resfriará.
14.¿ Dónde comieron los bocadillos y bebieron las bebidas? Comieron los bocadillos y bebieron la cerveza en el patio de Carlos.

23. THE IMPERATIVE OR COMMAND MODE 1- "TÚ"- SINGULAR INFORMAL.

PRACTICE A:

1. ¡Trabaja ahora!
2. ¡Estudia hoy!
3. ¡Compra el coche!
4. ¡Espera aquí!
5. ¡Bebe esto!
6. ¡Corre rápido!
7. ¡Aprende todo!
8. ¡Canta para él!
9. ¡Baila en la mesa!

10. ¡Vive hoy!
11. ¡Escribe aquí!
12. ¡Come más!
13. ¡Lee eso!
14. ¡Toma el dinero!

PRACTICE B:

1. ¡No mires la casa!
2. ¡No cantes esa canción!
3. ¡No corras en el pasillo!
4. ¡No estudies aléman, estudia español!
5. ¡No pienses tanto!
6. ¡No creas todo!
7. ¡No abras la puerta!
8. ¡No leas mi agenda!
9. ¡No bailes con él!
10. ¡No esperes toda la noche!
11. ¡No pagues nada todavía!
12. ¡No practiques toda la noche!
13. ¡No llegues tarde!
14. ¡No bebas demasiado!

24. IMPERATIVE "TÚ"- IRREGULAR VERBS.

PRACTICE A:

1. ¡Pon el dinero aqui!
2. ¡Díme todo!
3. ¡Hazme una taza de té!
4. ¡Sal de la casa ahora!
5. ¡Ven a la fiesta temprano!
6. ¡Sé bueno!
7. ¡Ve a las tiendas!
8. ¡Ten el rojo!
9. ¡No pongas las llaves allí!
10. ¡No digas nada!
11. ¡No hagas la cena ahora!
12. ¡No salgas de esta habitación!
13. ¡No vengas más!
14. ¡No seas tonto!

15. ¡No vayas al colegio hoy!
16. ¡No tengas más animales!

25. PLACEMENT OF OBJECT PRONOUNS WITH THE IMPERATIVE.

PRACTICE A: (Audio 31)

1. ¡Cómpramela!
2. ¡Dáselo!
3. ¡Encuéntramelo ahora!
4. ¡Dile!
5. ¡Mándaselo!
6. ¡Escríbenoslo!
7. ¡Véndeselo!
8. ¡Házmelo!
9. ¡Ábrenoslo!
10. ¡Házselo!
11. ¡No lo toques!
12. ¡No se lo haces!
13. ¡No se la pagues!
14. ¡No se lo leas!
15. ¡No me lo cierres!
16. ¡No se la hagas!
17. ¡No nos lo dejes!
18. ¡No me lo traigas!
19. ¡No se lo cocines!
20. ¡No me olvides!

26. THE IMPERATIVE OR COMMAND MODE 2- "VOSOTROS"- PLURAL INFORMAL.

PRACTICE A:

1. ¡Subid las escaleras!
2. ¡Traédmelo!
3. ¡Cepillaos los dientes!
4. ¡Sed agradables con ellos!
5. ¡Id a la cama!
6. ¡Llevadlo a casa!
7. ¡Escribidlos!

8. ¡Lávaos las manos!
9. ¡Borradlo!
10. ¡Apagadlo!
11. ¡Encendedlo!
12. ¡Dormios!
13. ¡Cerrad la puerta!
14. ¡Pagad la cuenta!
15. ¡Aféitaos!
16. ¡Id!
17. ¡Tenedlo!
18. ¡Dúchaos!
19. ¡Estad felices!
20. ¡Decidme!

PRACTICE B:

1. ¡No os vayáis!
2. ¡No os paréis!
3. ¡No os repitáis!
4. ¡No nos traigáis nada!
5. ¡No lo pongáis allí!
6. ¡No me odiáis!
7. ¡No lleguéis tardes!
8. ¡No los toquéis!
9. ¡No le digáis nada!
10. ¡No vayáis todavía!
11. ¡No seáis tan tacaños!
12. ¡No sepáis todo!

27. PRACTICE THE IMPERATIVE.

PRACTICE A:

1. We can´t sleep at night.
2. Lately I have put on a lot of weight.
3. I feel lonely at times.
4. We spend a lot of money and we can´t help it.
5. My boyfriend wants to split up with me.
6. I don´t know what to buy for my mother for her birthday.
7. We don´t like our job in the office.
8. I have lost my wallet.

9. I don´t know what to do this weekend.
10. I have a cold.
11. Our dog is very agressive.
12. I want to learn Spanish
13. We don´t want to live in the City any more.
14. I would like to buy a new car.
15. Our child is very naughty.
16. I don´t like my friend´s boyfriend.
17. I never have enough money.
18. I want to live in another country.
19. We never have time for anything.
20. I want a new car but not very expensive.

PRACTICE B: FREE ANSWERS.

29. PRONOUN PRACTICE

PRACTICE A:

SUBJECT PRONOUNS	
ENGLISH	SPANISH
I	yo
you	tú
he/ she/ it	El/ ella
we	nosotros/as
you	vosotros
they	ellos/ellas

POSSESSIVE PRONOUNS	
ENGLISH	SPANISH
my	mi/s
your	tu/s
his/her	Su/
our	nuestro/a/os/as
your	vuestro/a/os/as
their	su/s

REFLEXIVE PRONOUNS	
ENGLISH	SPANISH
myself	me
yourself	te
him/herself	se
ourselves	nos
yourselves	os
themselves	se

DIRECT OBJECT PRONOUNS	
ENGLISH	SPANISH
me	me
you	te
him/her/it	lo/la
us	nos
you(s)	os
them	los/las

INDIRECT OBJECT PRONOUNS	
ENGLISH	SPANISH
me	me
you	te
him/her	le
us	nos
you(s)	os
them	les

"PARA" PRONOUNS	
ENGLISH	SPANISH
me	mí
you	tí
him/her/it	él/ella
us	nos
you(s)	os
them	ellos/ellas

PRACTICE B:

1. Se levanta cada mañana a las ocho.
2. Fuimos al centro commercial ayer para comprarnos un regalo.
3. Lo vendieron la semana pasada..
4. Me he lavado el pelo tres veces esta semana.
5. ¿Quieres vender tu coche?
6. El vestido en la ventana es perfecto para ella.
7. Tiene un regalo para tí.
8. Nos acostamos a las once anoche.
9. Los ví ayer. I saw them yesterday.
10. Anteayer nos dijo la verdad.

PRACTICE C: FREE ANSWERS

30. PRACTICE OF PERSONAL PRONOUNS

PRACTICE A:

1. Él preguntará/ Pedirá al policia la dirección.
   Se la preguntará/ pedirá.

2. La abuela ha leído un cuento a su nieta.
   La abuela se lo ha leído.

3. La madre ponia el abrigo en su hijo.
   La madre se lo ponía.

4. El vendedor había envuelto el libro para nosotros.
   El vendedor nos lo había envuelto.

5. Hice una pregunta a la profesora.
   Se la hice.

6. Siempre compraban flores para su madre.
   Siempre se las compraban.

7. Recomendamos este hotel para vosotros.
   Os lo recomendamos.

8. ¿Devolverás el libro a mí mañana?
   ¿Me lo devolverás mañana?

31. SER AND ESTAR MIXED TENSES.

PRACTICE A:

1. PRESENT TENSE

ENGLISH-TO BE	SER	ESTAR
I am	soy	estoy
You are	eres	estás
He/she it is	es	está
We are	somos	estamos
You(s) are	sois	estáis
They are	son	están

2. PRESENT PERFECT

ENGLISH-TO BE	SER	ESTAR
I have been	he sido	he estado
You have been	has sido	has estado
He/she/it has been	ha sido	ha estado
We have been	hemos sido	hemos estado
You(s) have been	habéis sido	habéis estado
They have been	han sido	han estado

3. PRETERITE

ENGLISH-TO BE	SER	ESTAR
I was	fui	estuve
You were	fuiste	estuviste
He/she/it was	fue	estuvo
We were	fuimos	estuvimos
You(s) were	fuisteis	estuvisteis
They were	fueron	estuvieron

4. IMPERFECT

ENGLISH-TO BE	SER	ESTAR
I was/was being/used to be	era	estaba
You were/were being/ used to be	eras	estabas
He/she/it Was/was being/used to be	era	estaba
We were/were being/ used to be	éramos	estabamos
You(s) were/were being/ used to be	erais	estabais
They were/were being/ used to be	eran	estaban

5. FUTURE

ENGLISH-TO BE	SER	ESTAR
I wil be	seré	estaré
You wil be	serás	estarás
He/she/it wil be	será	estará
We wil be	seremos	estaremos
You(s) wil be	seréis	estaréis
They wil be	serán	estarán

6. CONDITIONAL.

ENGLISH-TO BE	SER	ESTAR
I would be	sería	estaría
You would be	serías	estarías
He/she/it would be	sería	estaría
We would be	seríamos	estaríamos
You(s) would be	seríais	estaríais
They would be	serían	estarían

PRACTICE B: FREE ANSWERS

PRACTICE C:

1. (Ella) será la primera presidenta de los Estados Unidos
2. La mesa es cuadrada.
3. Han sido profesores durante/ por veinte años.
4. Nunca estaban en clase.
5. Son de España.
6. ¿Quién es Juan?
7. Nunca he sido su amigo.
8. El examen estuve en en colegio y fue muy difícil.

9. Cada semana eran más caros.
10. ¿Cuándo es la clase?
11. Hemos estado en Inglaterra.
12. Sería muy buen precio, pero no funciona.
13. ¿Estás cansado/a?
14. ¿Estáis felices?
15. Ella está en el jardín.
16. Han estado enfermos.
17. He estado muy triste.
18. París está en Francia.
19. Los niños están tristes.
20. Serán muy altos en cinco años.
21. ¿De dónde eres?
22. ¿Dónde han estado?
23. Estuvieron listos a ir a las seis.
24. La pelota es roja.
25. Jordi y María han estado muy cansados hoy.
26. ¿Cómo estás?
27. ¿Cómo es Pedro?
28. Cada lunes las colas esran largas.
29. Los viernes estaba en el trabajo hasta las ocho.
30. Los gatos han estado en la terraza toda la mañana.
31. La casa está sucia.
32. José siempre ha sido un hombre muy guapo.
33. María y Belen son rubias.
34. Manuel y Begoña han sido abogados en la ciudad desde hace 2005.
35. Ha sido mi mejor amigo por diez años.
36. ¿Cuándo es la clases de español?
37. La boda fue el sábado.
38. ¿Son españoles?
39. La comida estuvo en un restaurante en el centro de la ciudad. Fue buena.
40. En la boda, los cubiertos que estuvieron en la mesa eran de plata.
41. David era muy inteligente pero nunca estaba contento con nada.
42. En mil novecientos y noventa y nueve viví en Inglaterra y fui estudiante.
43. La última vez que estuve en Londrés tuve una experiencia terrible.
44. Fui Presidente del club por un año.
45. ¿Quién fue el ganador ayer?
46. Fue una fiesta terrible.
47. Fue mi mejor amiga por diez años.
48. ¿Cuándo fue la clase?

49. ¿Cómo estuvo Miguel ayer?
50. Cuando era niño siempre estaba en el parque.
51. El café en el restaurante ayer estuvo frio.
52. A las tres ya estuve/ estaba en casa.
53. Barecelona será una ciudad preciosa para visitar.
54. ¿Cómo era el padre de Carlos?
55. ¿Dónde estuviste/ estabas? Te estaba buscando.
56. Era actríz que me gustaba mucho.
57. ¿Estarás en Sevilla para Semana Santa?
58. ¿Dónde está mi coche?
59. Siempre estaban de buen humor y nos decían cuentos graciosos.
60. Estuve enfermo y no pude/ podía ir a la fiesta.
61. Quería comprar los zapatos perp eran caros.
62. ¿Por qué estuvo/ estaba él en ese coche?
63. Esta manzana está marrón.
64. Cuando estaba en España, era policia.
65. Cada lunes estaba enferma y no podía trabajar.
66. Los viernes las bebidas eran baratas.
67. Él estará allí a las cinco.
68. Cada semana estaba allí a su casa.
69. ¿Habéis sido estudiantes alguna vez?
70. Siempre era alta para su edad.
71. Las tiendas siempre estaban cerradas los domingos.
72. Nunca eran bailadores muy buenos.
73. Nunca estabais aquí cuando os necesitaba.
74. Yo nunca era estricto/a.
75. Nunca estaban en clase.
76. ¿Con quien/es estamos?
77. Una vez al mes él estaba/ estuvo feliz/ contento cuando ella estaba/ estuvo allí.
78. Estabais a menudo en la playa cuando estaba yo.
79. ¿Estuviste casado en 1996?
80. Cada año estaban abiertos más tarde.
81. Siempre has sido alto/a.
82. Estaría feliz, pero no tengo dinero.
83. Ella sería enfermera pero no le gusta el sangre.
84. Estarán muy enfadados.
85. Estarías allí, pero no hay más plazas.
86. Estaremos al/ en el hotel el sábado.
87. Mi casa vieja estaba en el centro del pueblo.

88. ¿Estarás en casa esta noche?
89. ¿Cuánto sería para dos adultos y dos niños?
90. Juan era muy alto y guapo.
91. Cada año las vacaciones eran más y más caras.
92. Pienso/ creo que será un partido bueno mañana.
93. Si vamos temprano, estaremos primeros en la cola.
94. Una vez al mes era cantante en un bar.
95. La mesa está sucía..
96. Él no estaría aquí, pero lo llamé ayer para invitarle.
97. Él será muy simpático.
98. ¿Estaríais contentos/ felices con el coche pequeño?
99. Serían tan ricos, pero perdieron todo su dinero en el casino.
100. Eso sería estupendo/ genial.

32. TRANSLATION FROM ENGISH TO SPANISH MIXED TENSES-"LA AVENTURA MÉXICANA DE JUAN PÉREZ".

PRACTICE A:

VERB	INFINITIVE	SPANISH	TENSE	PERSON
1. changed	To change	cambiar	preterite	3rd p.sing
2. decided	To decide	decidir	preterite	3rd p.sing
3. to buy	To buy	comprar	infinitive	
4. smiled	To smile	sonreir	preterite	3rd p.sing
5. said	To say	decir	preterite	3rd p.sing
6. have won	To win	ganar	pres.perfect	2nd p.sing
7. was	To be	estar	imperfect	3rd p.sing
8. he didn´t hesitate	To hesitate	vacilar	preterite	3rd p.sing
9. accepting	To accept	aceptar	infinitive	
10. he had	To have	tener	imperfect	3rd p.sing
11. wrote	To write	escribir	imperfect	3rd p.sing
12. had never left	To leave	salir	past perfect	3rd p.sing
13. he got on	To get on	subir	preterite	3rd p.sing
14. went off	To go off	irse	preterite	3rd p.sing
15. he arrived	To arrive	llegar	preterite	3rd p.sing
16. was waiting	To wait	esperar	imperfect	3rd p.sing
17. had never seen	To see	ver	past perfect	3rd p.sing
18. was	To be	estar	imperfect	3rd p.sing
19. were greeting	To greet	recibir	imperfect	3rd p.plur

20. were returning	To return	volver	imperfect	3rd p.sing
21. saw	To see	ver	preterite	3rd p.sing
22. saying	To say	decir	gerund	
23. he saw	To see	ver	preterite	3rd p.sing
24. he approached	To approach	acercarse	preterite	3rd p.sing
25. I am	To be	ser	present	1st p.sing
26. said	To say	decir	preterite	3rd p.sing
27. smiling	To smile	sonreir	gerund	
28. I am	To be	ser	present	1st p.sing
29. he replied	To reply	responder	preterite	3rd p.sing
30. she gave	To give	dar	preterite	3rd p.sing
31. he replied	To reply	responder	preterite	3rd p.sing
32. is	To be	ser	present	3rd p.sing
33. they left	To leave	salir	preterite	3rd p.plur
34. got into	To get into	subir	preterite	3rd p.plur
35. drove	To drive	conducir	preterite	3rd p.plur
36. lived	To live	vivir	imperfect	3rd p.sing
37. they arrived	To arrive	llegar	preterite	3rd p.plur
38. ran	To run	correr	preterite	3rd p.plur
39. to look	To look	mirar	infinitive	
40. laughing	To laugh	reirse	gerund	
41. pointing	To point	señalar	gerund	
42. turned off	To turn off	apagar	preterite	3rd p.sing
43. turned	To turn	girarse	preterite	3rd p.sing
44. smiled	To smile	sonreir	preterite	3rd p.sing
45. said	To say	decir	preterite	3rd p.sing
46. was beginning	To begin	empezar	imperfect	3rd p.sing

PRACTICE B:

La vida de Juan Pérez, un español de Salamanca, cambió el día que decidió a comprar una televisión en El Corte Inglés. La suerte lo sonreió con un trozo de papel escondido dentro que dijo: "ENHORABUENA- HAS GANADO UN VIAJE A MÉXICO PARA DOS PERSONAS". Aunque Juan estaba soltero, no vaciló ni un momento en aceptar el premio. En México tenía familia lejano que todavía le escribía y Juan nunca había salido de Salamanca en su vida entera. Un día bonito subió en un avión y se fue a Cancún.

Cuándo llegó al aeropuerto su sobrina Juanita lo esperaba. Juan nunca la había visto menos en las fotos. El aeropuerto estaba lleno de aficionados al fútbol que recibían al equipo méxicano con entusiasmo, que volvía victorioso de una gira por Europa. Entre la gente, Juan vio a una chica muy morena y guapa, con los brazos elevados y un cartel diciendo simplemente "JUAN". Tan pronto como vio el cartel, se la acercó.

"Soy Juanita", dijo ella, sonriendo.
"Y yo soy Juan", respondió él.

Le dio un beso en la mejilla y él respondió con dos, como es costumbre en España. Salieron del aeropuerto y subieron en un coche amarillo, después condujeron al pueblo donde vivía Juanita. Cuando llegaron, muchos niños corrieron al coche para mirar al desconocido, riéndose y señalando. Juanita apagó el motor, se giró la cabeza hacia Juan, sonreió, y dijo: "Bienvenido a México".
La aventura méxicana de Juan Pérez empezaba…

PRACTICE C:

1. ¿Qué pasó cuando Juan Pérez decidió a comprar una televisión en El Corte Inglés? Su vida cambió.
2. ¿De dónde era? Era de Salamanca.
3. ¿Qué encontró adentro? Encontró un trozo de papel.
4. ¿Qué había ganado? Había ganado un viaje a México para dos personas.
5. ¿Vaciló en aceptar el premio? No, no vaciló ni un momento.
6. ¿Estaba casado? No, no estaba casado.
7. ¿Qué tenía en México? Tenía familia lejana.
8. ¿Que hizo un día bonito? Subió en un avión y se fue a Cancún.
9. ¿Quién lo esperaba en el aeropuerto? Su sobrina Juanita lo esperaba.
10. ¿La había visto Juan alguna vez? No la había visto menos en las fotos.
11. ¿De dónde volvía el equipo méxicano? Volvía victorioso de una gira de Europa.
12. ¿A quién vio entre la gente? Vio a una chica morena y muy guapa.
13. ¿Qué hizo tan pronto como vio el cartel? Se la acercó. (a la chica).
14. ¿Dónde lo besó? Lo besó en la mejilla.
15. ¿Qué pasó cuando llegaron en el pueblo de Juanita? Muchos niños corrieron al coche para mirar al desconocido.
16. ¿Qué dijo Juanita cuando apagó el motor y se giró la cabeza hacia él? Dijo: "Bienvenido a México".

33. QUERIDA PILI

PRACTICE A:

	VERB	INFINITIVE	ENGLISH	TENSE	PERSON
1.	Tengo que	Tener que	To have to	present	1st p. sing
2.	decir	decir	To	infinitive	
3.	fue	ser	To be	preterite	3rd p. sing
4.	mandar	mandar	To send	infinitive	
5.	Hicieron	hacer	To do	preterite	3rd p. plural
6.	Estoy	estar	To be	present	1st p. sing
7.	pasando	pasar	To pass	"ing"	
8.	he escrito	escribir	To write	pres.perfect	1st p. sing
9.	contar	contar	To tell	infinitive	
10.	sé	saber	To know	present	1st p. sing
11.	haré	hacer	To do	future	1st p. sing
12.	ves	ver	To see	present	2nd p. sing
13.	estoy	estar	To be	present	1st p. sing
14.	usando	usar	To use	"ing"	
15.	escribir	escribir	To write	infinitive	
16.	Me llevo	llevarse	To get on with	present	1st p. sing
17.	juro	jurar	To swear	present	1st p. sing
18.	hacemos	hacer	To do	present	1st p.plural
19.	pasar	pasar	To spend/pass	infinitive	
20.	descanso	descansar	To relax	present	1st p. sing
21.	parece	parecer	To seem	present	3rd p. sing
22.	duermo	dormir	To sleep	present	1st p. sing
23.	tenga	tener	To have	Subjunctive (see Level 4!!)	3rd p. sing
24.	ver	ver	To see	infinitive	
25.	fumo	fumar	To smoke	present	1st p. sing
26.	crees	creer	To think/believe	present	2nd p. sing
27.	es	ser	To be	present	3rd p. sing
28.	Duermo	dormir	To sleep	present	1st p. sing
29.	me levanto	levantarse	To get up	present	1st p. sing
30.	desayuno	desayunar	To have breakfast	present	1st p. sing
31.	salgo	salir	To go out	present	1st p. sing

BREAK THE LANGUAGE BARRIER LEVEL 3
WWW.ELPRINCIPECENTRE.COM
info@elprincipecentre.org

32. paso	pasar	To pass/spend	present	1st p. sing
33. leyendo	leer	To read	"ing"	
34. se levantan	levantarse	To get up	present	3rd p. plural
35. tienen	tener	To have	present	3rd p. plural
36. voy	ir	To go	present	1st p. sing
37. contar	contar	To tell	infinitive	
38. han gustado	gustar	To like(please)	Pres.perfect	3rd p. plural
39. fuimos	ir	To go	preterite	1st p. plural
40. habían organizado	organizar	To organize	Past perfect	3rd p.plural
41. vino	venir	To come	preterite	3rd p. sing
42. Compramos	comprar	To buy	preterite	1st p. plural
43. cargamos	cargar	To load up	preterite	1st p. plural
44. Sabes	saber	To know	present	2nd p. sing
45. es	ser	To be	present	3rd p. sing
46. tuvimos	tener	To have	preterite	1st p. plural
47. estuvimos	estar	To estar	preterite	1st p. plural
48. reparando	reparar	To repair/fix	"ing"	1st p. sing
49. llegamos	llegar	To arrive	preterite	1st p. plural
50. preparamos	preparar	To prepare	preterite	1st p. plural
51. empezamos	empezar	To empezar	preterite	1st p. plural
52. asar	asar	To roast	infinitive	1st p. plural
53. bailamos	bailar	To dance	preterite	1st p. plural
54. charlamos	charlar	To chat	preterite	1st p. plural
55. llegamos	llegar	To arrive	preterite	1st p. plural
56. logró	lograr	To manage	preterite	3rd p. sing
57. arrancar	arrancar	To start	infinitive	
58. tuvo	tener	To have	preterite	3rd p. sing
59. venir	venir	To come	infinitive	
60. recoger	recoger	To collect	infinitive	
61. se enfadó	enfadarse	To get angry	preterite	3rd p. sing
62. llevaron	llevar	To take	preterite	3rd p. plural
63. ver	ver	To see	infinitive	present
64. había visto	ver	To see	past perfect	3rd p. sing
65. contaba	contar	To tell	imperfect	3rd p. sing
66. vivía	vivir	To live	imperfect	3rd p. sing
67. trabajaba	trabajar	To work	imperfect	3rd p. sing
68. Viajaba	viajar	To travel	imperfect	3rd p. sing
69. hacía	hacer	To do	imperfect	3rd p. sing
70. viene	venir	To come	present	3rd p. sing

71. llevarán	llevar	To take	preterite	3rd p. plural
72. tengo	tengo	To have	present	1st p. sing
73. ir	ir	To go	infinitive	
74. estará	estar	To be	future	3rd p. sing
75. Nos quedaremos	quedar	To stay	future	3rd p.plural
76. contaré	contar	To tell	future	1st p. sing
77. dejo	dejar	To leave	present	1st p. sing
78. estamos	estar	To be	present	1st p.plural
79. salir	salir	To leave	infinitive	

PRACTICE B:

Dear Pili

I have to tell you that it was a great idea of my parents to send me here to Girona to my aunt and uncle´s house. They did well because I am having a great time. Of course I haven´t written to my parents yet to tell them!
I don´t know if I will although, as you see, I am using my aunt´s computer to write some emails.
 I get on very well with my cousins and I swear to you we do something interesting every day. Apart from having a good time, I also relax a lot. It seems to me that I sleep much better here tan at home, maybe it has something to do with the air, and that now I don´t smoke. Don´t you believe me? Well it´s true.
I sleep well, I get up quite late and normally I have breakfast and go out to the garden, with a book and my Ipad. There I spend a couple of hours reading. My cousins José and María get up at 8 because the both have exams in three weeks. Poor things!!
I´m going to tell you about some things I have liked. Last Tuesday we went to a barbecue in a nearby small village. Some friends of José had organized it. Rafael came with his girlfriend. We bought the food and all the drinks in the morning and loaded up Josés car. Do you know hoew old his car is? Well. We had a puncture on the road and we were half an hour reparing it.
At last we we arrived, we prepared the salads and some enormous tortillas and we started to roast the meat. Then we danced and chatted until 4 o´clock in the morning. We did not arrive home until the early hours because José didn´t manage to start the car and my uncle had to come for us. Luckily, he didn´t get angry!!!

Last Saturday my aunt and uncle took me to see an uncle of mine I had not seen for nearly ten years. He was telling me stories of when he lived/ used to live in the United States and he worked/ used to work for an International bank. He travelled/ used to travel all over the world and did/ used to do many interesting things. Next weekend they will take me to an Estopa concert. I am really looking forward to it. The concert will be in Barcelona and we will stay there 2 nights, I will tell you all about it in my next email.

Ok, I Will leave you because we are about to leave for the market. Give my regards to your parents and brother.

A big hug- Mercedes

PRACTICE C:

1. ¿Quién mandó Pili a a Girona? Sus padres.
2. ¿(Lo) está pasando(lo) bien? Si, (lo) está pasando (bien)
3. ¿Ha escrito a sus padres todavía? No.
4. ¿Por qué piensa que duerme major allí que en la casa? Quizás tiene algo que ver con el aire, y que ya no fumo.
5. ¿Qué hace normalmente después de levantarse? Normalmente desayuna y sale al jardín con un libro y su Ipod.
6. ¿Por qué se levantan los primos a las 8? Porque los dos tienen exámenes dentro de tres semanas.
7. ¿Adónde fueron el mares pasado? Fueron a una barbacoa.
8. ¿Quiénes la habían organizado? Unos amigos de José
9. ¿Qué pasó en la carretera? Tuvieron un pinchazo.
10. ¿Hasta qué hora bailaron y charlaron? Hasta las cuatro de la mañana.
11. ¿Por qué no llegaron a casa hasta la madrugada el día siguiente? José no logró arrancar el coche y su tío tuvo que venir para recogerles.
12. ¿Adónde la llevaron sus tios el sábado pasado? A ver un tio suyo que no había visto en más de diez años.
13. ¿Dónde trabajaba el tio? Para un banco internacional.
14. ¿Adónde la llevarán sus tios el sábado que viene? A un concierto de Estopa en Barcelona.
15. ¿Cuánto tiempo se quedará allí? Dos noches.
16. ¿Qué va a hacer ahora? Salir para el mercadillo.

34. PREPOSITIONS

1. Prepositions that show a relationship between people and/or things:

PRACTICE A:

1. Era persona sin problemas.
2. Ella siempre hablaba de su novio.
3. Siempre hablaré contra la violencia.
4. Según mi mejor amigo/a, fue/era la mejor película que jámas había visto.
5. Además de flores, su marido le compra chocolate cada semana.
6. Nos gusta todo aquí menos la vista.
7. Querían patatas fritas con todo.
8. Compré un libro de la historia de España.
9. ¿Puedes darme arroz en vez de pasta por favor?

2. Prepositions of place:

PRACTICE B: FREE ANSWER

3. Prepositions of movement:

PRACTICE C:

1. Siempre corria alredor del lago cada mañana.
2. Caminaremos por la calle principal hasta Correos.
3. El policía buscaba por toda la casa.
4. Siempre tengo que mirar hacia delante al futuro, no hacía detrás hacia el pasado.
5. Condujeron hacia el rio y después anduvieron a lo largo del camino.
6. Ella miré más allá del árbol y pudo/ podía ver la casa.
7. Los cangrejos andan de lado.
8. No irá más allá de este punto.

4. Prepositions of origin and destination:

PRACTICE D:

1. No pude ir ayer por el tiempo.
2. He leído todos los libros de Stephen King.

3. Este regalo es para ti.
4. Iremos al concierto el sábado.
5. No compró el coche por el precio.
6. Elegimos esta alfombra para el salón.
7. Estas tazas son de Japón.
8. Los pájaros volarían hacia el mar.

5. Prepositions of time:

PRACTICE E:

1. No tienes que estar aqui hasta mañana.
2. Necesitamos reparar el coche antes del invierno.
3. Ha hecho mucho calor desde el principio de junio.
4. Quería creer en la vida después de la muerte.
5. ¿Qué vas a hacer durante el verano?
6. Me dijeron la verdad antes.
7. Normalmente me hace un té durante los anuncios.
8. Estuve en Portugal por/ durante casi 2 años.
9. Trabajabamos de lunes a sábado sin pausa.
10. Veré/ moraré la película y cenaré después.

35. CONVERSATION TRANSLATION PALOMA AND JUAN

PRACTICE A:

JUAN: El sábado me levanté muy tarde porque estuve tan agotado después de trabajar tan duro durante la semana.
PALOMA: ¿Qué llamas tarde?
JUAN: Las doce y media/ treinta o la una. Fue casi la hora de comer. Mi esposa/ mujer no estuvo muy contenta/ fel´z porque quería ir de compras conmigo por la mañana.
PALOMA: ¿Entonces tuvisteis que ir por la tarde?
JUAN: Por supuesto. Y fue interminable, porque las tiendas estuvieron llenas. Entonces cuando volvemos, mi mujer/esposa preparó una cena rápida y nos sentamos a mirar/ ver la televisión hasta las once y media/ treinta. ¿Qué hiciste tú?
PALOMA: Fui a una boda el sábado. Un primo mio se casaba.
JUAN: ¿Lo pasaste bien?

PALOMA: Sí, estuvo bien/ fue bueno. La comida fue muy buena y las bebidas tambien, claro. Había música y baliando hasta las tres de la mañana/ madrugada.
JUAN: Y domingo, ¿qué hiciste?
PALOMA: Nada importante. Dormir, leer el periódico, y mirar la tele. ¿Y tú?
JUAN: Más o menos igual/ el mismo como tú.

36. EMAILS

PRACTICE A: FREE ANSWERS

www.ingramcontent.com/pod-product-compliance
Lightning Source LLC
Chambersburg PA
CBHW081346040426
42450CB00015B/3327